STUDYING FILMS

STUDYING WALTZ WITH BASHIR
Giulia Miller

Acknowledgements

Thanks to Hannah Ewence and Helen Spurling for all their helpful comments, and for allowing me to re-publish a section of my essay 'Ari Folman's Other War: Animating and Erasing the Holocaust in *Waltz with Bashir*'.

Dedication

For Neil and Noa.

First published in 2017 by
Auteur, 24 Hartwell Crescent, Leighton Buzzard LU7 1NP
www.auteur.co.uk

Designed and set by Nikki Hamlett at Cassels Design www.casselsdesign.co.uk

British Library Cataloguing-in-Publication Data
A catalogue record for this book is available from the British Library

ISBN: paperback 978-1-911325-15-4
ISBN: ebook 978-1-911325-16-1

Contents

Chapter One: *Waltz with Bashir*: Why Does it Matter?

July 2014, the summer before I began writing this book, saw one of the most horrific episodes in the history of the Middle East conflict. Following the kidnapping and murder of three Israeli teenagers by members of the Islamist militant group Hamas, came a brutal revenge attack that triggered a fifty-day war between Israel and Hamas-controlled Gaza, a 146-square-mile strip of Palestinian land located on Israel's south western border next to Egypt. The war resulted in the death of over 2000 Palestinians and sixty-six Israelis. Throughout July and August 2014 there were constant news reports detailing the exact number of airstrikes, rockets and ground invasions, the number of buildings destroyed and the bombing of underground tunnels leading from Gaza into Southern Israel. Awareness of the conflict was global and reactions to it could be found all over the world's media.

Now almost a month later as I ponder the function and value of a film such as Ari Folman's animated documentary *Waltz with Bashir* I am struck by the yawning gap between global consciousness of Israeli politics and that of Israeli culture. Ironically, one of the responses to the recent Gaza crisis was to suggest a cultural boycott on Israel and I wonder how many people would have understood what this might involve. Whilst this is understandable with regards to some cultural forms such as fine art or theatre, which don't always travel well, it is more surprising with regards to the film and TV industry. Although many TV fans might be aware that TV favourites, such as *Homeland* and *In Treatment*, are actually American versions of the Israeli original, Israeli cinema does not pull the same cultural punch as other so-called world cinemas. There are certainly all sorts of possible reasons for this, including a comparative lack of film funding in Israel and the fact that the main language spoken is Hebrew, which isn't spoken anywhere else in the world (unlike for example French, Portuguese or Spanish). Furthermore, it does not, for whatever reason evoke the same enthusiasm as other languages such as Japanese, Russian, Chinese, or Swedish, all of which are popular alternatives to English both as subjects of study and as objects of historical and cultural interest. Consequently, until recently, even devoted world cinema goers would have been hard pushed to name an Israeli film or director.

The glaring exception to this rule is of course Ari Folman's animated documentary *Waltz with Bashir* (2008), which struck a chord on the international art house scene and was a roaring success, winning a Golden Globe award for Best Foreign Language Film, and ranking number 34 in *Empire* magazine's 'The 100 Best Films of World Cinema' in 2010. The director, Ari Folman, who was already an established director and screen writer in Israel, became famous worldwide. With the release of his most recent film *The Congress* (2013), which stars Hollywood actors Harvey Keitel, Jon Hamm and Robin Wright, he might now even be considered mainstream, thus potentially undermining his niche status as director of provocative independent cinema.

The aim of this book is to get to the heart of why *Waltz with Bashir* was such a phenomenon and to question if it is still as significant now as it was when it was first released in 2008, and if so, how. Prior to the discussion I would like to give a brief précis of the film and outline the aims of each of the six chapters.

Plot synopsis

Waltz with Bashir is narrated by a middle-aged Israeli film maker, allegedly Folman himself (Folman served in the Israeli army when he was nineteen), who is trying to recall his experiences as a soldier during the 1982 Lebanon War, and more specifically, his role during the Sabra and Shatila massacres, when more than 1,700 Palestinians were murdered by the Lebanese Christian Phalangist militia. The attack was carried out, over the course of three days, in revenge for the assassination of Lebanon's newly elected Christian president Bashir Gemayel, which was blamed on the Palestinians. The Israel Defence Forces (IDF) provided military cover for the Phalangists and was therefore complicit in the massacre.

The film begins, cryptically, with a pack of rabid black and grey dogs, with yellow eyes and teeth, running through Tel Aviv's Rothschild Boulevard, knocking over tables, terrorising pedestrians, but all of them running together in the same direction, as though hypnotised. Eventually, they stop at a building and the viewer follows the animals' menacing gaze upwards to a window where a man is standing. We then switch to a dimly-lit bar where an older version of this man is sitting at a small table with Folman; the year is 2006 and the man's name is Boaz Rein-Buskila. Over beers, shots, and cigarettes, we learn that Boaz was also a soldier in Lebanon in 1982 and that these dogs, twenty-six in total, have been haunting his dreams every night for the past two and a half years. It turns out that one of Boaz's jobs in the army was to dispense of Palestinian guard dogs. He slaughtered twenty-six in total and the trauma has never left him.

Has Boaz ever seen a therapist, asks Folman, helpfully. No, replies Boaz, but he called Folman because he thinks he might help. After all, aren't films a kind of therapy, and hasn't Folman been dealing with personal issues through film his whole career? Folman looks totally perplexed. Boaz then asks him the million dollar question: don't you have any flashbacks from Lebanon? The response is a resounding no – Folman doesn't remember anything about that period in his life. Then, that night, for the first time in over twenty years, he has his first flashback about the Sabra and Shatila massacres, and this triggers his desire to remember more. Where was he on the night of the massacres? What was he doing? What did he see?

The rest of the film shows Folman carrying out a series of interviews with friends and various professionals – a psychiatrist, a journalist, and an army general –as he tries to piece together what actually happened those many years ago. Amongst the interview scenes there are three recurring visions in which Folman and his comrades emerge naked out of the water and walk towards a city. The vision always ends with Palestinian women running towards them seemingly crying. Apart from the music in the background there is no sound in these recurring scenes.

In the film's final scene, which is coincidentally the only scene to use live footage, we see a continuation of Folman's recurring vision, but this time we see the animated Palestinian women with live sound in the background. This eventually morphs into live visual footage of the same women crying and repeatedly screaming in Arabic: 'My son, my son!' 'Take photos, take photos!' 'Where are the Arabs, where are the Arabs?' The Arabic is not translated in the subtitles. Much has been said about Folman's decision to switch from animation to live footage at this precise moment, and I shall discuss the possible implications of the switch later in Chapter Three. The crucial point is that since the live footage is more or less identical to Folman's three recurring visions it does not simply mark a moment of recollection. Rather it also marks a moment when the trauma Folman has repressed finally comes to the surface. The live footage represents the point when Folman is suddenly hit by the full force of his experiences. This is reinforced by the introduction of sound. It is as though everything in Folman's mind has been muffled but now there is immense clarity.

In addition to Folman's personal amnesia and confusion about Lebanon, there is a further narrative layer that deals with collective memory: halfway through the film, during a second visit to his friend, Ori Sivan, the subject of the Holocaust (also known as the Shoah: the systematic slaughter of six million Jews conducted by Adolf Hitler and the National Socialist Party during the Second World War) comes up. Sivan suggests that Folman's intense desire to find out what went on in the Sabra and Shatila camps, stems from Folman's need to understand what went on in the 'other' camps. It is at this point in the film we learn that Folman's parents were at Auschwitz; Sivan is therefore implying that Folman's personal investigation into the Lebanon War is motivated by an unconscious wish to deal with the Shoah. I think that the tension between the two investigations – one conscious, one apparently unconscious – is maintained throughout the film and that this is made possible by the use of animation. I shall discuss this in greater detail later on in the book.

Studying Waltz with Bashir is divided into six chapters. This first, introductory chapter will provide a general overview of the film, its production and its contexts.

Chapter Two will look at the film's form, asking the question: is *Waltz with Bashir* an animated work of fiction, or an animated documentary? Or even a combination of both? The film was never originally promoted as a documentary; the original Hebrew movie poster simply gives the film's title, whilst the English language version says in small print 'based on a true story'. Nevertheless, critically speaking, it has been treated as a documentary, winning best feature-length film by the International Documentary Association in 2008 and Best Documentary by the Writers Guild of America in 2009.[1] It has also been praised for accurately portraying the more unreliable psychological state of the traumatised soldier through animated dreams and flashbacks. This means that critical reception of *Waltz with Bashir* has retrospectively caused it to be redefined as 'animated documentary' (rather than animated drama based on a true story etc). The distinction between how the film was originally promoted and how it became to be defined is crucial; if *Waltz with Bashir* had been initially advertised as a documentary concerning Israel's role during the Sabra and Shatila massacres, then the viewers' expectations would have been entirely different.

The potential tension between the two modes –drama and documentary –is clear: the term 'drama' denotes fiction whilst 'documentary' suggests an honest and truthful investigation of, or exposition of, an individual's experience of a real life event.[2] Even if it is the account of one person, the viewer expects authenticity. In the case of *Waltz with Bashir* the use of the term 'documentary' implies that both Folman and the characters he interviews are describing their version of events as truthfully as possible.

The question I think is most pertinent to this study is: if it is documentary, a quest for truth, then what exactly does Folman achieve in *Waltz with Bashir* through animation? If it is an animated drama then why is it structured around interviews? What then is the function and effect of the film's form and how should it be interpreted by the film's audience: as a personal meditation on war, as confession, as denial, as political commentary, or as historical revisionism? I shall consider all these possibilities in Chapter Two.

Chapter Three is related to the previous chapter and is concerned specifically with the film's narrative structure. In particular, this chapter reflects on the differences between story and plot, as defined by David Bordwell and Kristin Thompson in their seminal text *Film Art: an Introduction*, and looks at how information is revealed to the audience. *Waltz with Bashir* is ordered around ten animated interview scenes which allegedly took place in 2006. The interviews are carried out as part of an investigation to help the film's narrator-protagonist, Ari Folman, overcome his amnesia about his role during the First Lebanon War. The final scene, which uses live news footage of the Sabra and Shatila camps, appears to mark the moment when Folman is hit by the full emotional force of his memories. The juxtaposition of live footage with total recall suggests that the film moves from unreliable or 'false' memory to 'real' truth. This chapter analyses this narrative arc in detail and shows how it can be interpreted in different ways.

The fourth chapter considers *Waltz with Bashir* within the broader context of non-animated and animated war films, e.g. *Apocalypse Now* (Francis Ford Coppola, 1979), *Barefoot Gen* (Mori Masaki, 1983), *When the Wind Blows* (Jimmy Murakami, 1986) and *Grave of the Fireflies* (Isao Takahata, 1988). The chapter will also look briefly at five other Israel films that deal with the subject of Lebanon: *Ricochets* (Eli Cohen, 1986), *Cherry Season* (Haim Bouzaglo, 1991); *Cup Final* (Eran Riklis, 1991); *Beaufort* (Joseph Cedar, 2007); *Lebanon* (Samuel Maoz, 2009). These films, however, use more conventional modes of narrative fiction filmmaking rather than animation or documentary, and this is one of the reasons why *Waltz with Bashir* stands out as a unique engagement with the topic.

Chapter Five looks at *Waltz with Bashir* within the context of the Holocaust. The eighties and nineties marked the emergence of second-generation Israeli cinema specifically produced by children of Holocaust survivors.[3] These second-generation films, whilst not explicitly addressing the subject of war, often critiqued the Zionist project (the move to establish a home for the Jews in Palestine), intimating that it had simply replaced the trauma of the Holocaust with a new and different kind of Israeli trauma. Ari Folman, who is also a child of survivors, began making films during this period. This chapter therefore looks at *Waltz with Bashir* as an example of second-generation film making and as a film that explicitly deals with Lebanon, but implicitly engages with events of the Second World War. The final chapter analyses primary sources such as newspapers and magazines to discuss the film's reception and consider some of the issues associated with world cinema.

Waltz with Bashir: Background

Folman's oeuvre as writer and director of television is extensive, and before making *Waltz with Bashir* he had already written and directed several successful TV dramas and documentaries including *Comfortably Numb* (*Sha'anan Si*, 1991) which won the Israeli Academy Award for Best Documentary.[4] His work as a writer and director of feature length films is considerably less extensive: before *Waltz with Bashir* Folman wrote and directed *Saint Clara* (*Klara Hakadosha*, 1996) and *Made in Israel* (2001) and more recently he has written and directed the partially animated science fiction fantasy *The Congress* (2013). There are, not surprisingly, striking similarities between these films and what I think is notable is that *Waltz with Bashir* seems to be a natural continuation, or synthesis even, of *Saint Clara* and *Made in Israel*. The main difference is their reception: Folman's first two feature length films gained only moderate recognition and this was limited to Israel; as we know, his third film became an international triumph. Meanwhile, *The Congress*, released in 2013, has not enjoyed the same success as *Waltz with Bashir* in spite of the fact that it is also partially animated and much was expected of it. In this chapter I shall focus on comparing the first three films: *Saint Clara*, *Made in Israel* and *Waltz with Bashir*. What stood out in *Waltz with Bashir* to make it so successful? One of the principal goals of this book is to provide an answer to this question. Let's look first at some of the three films' common characteristics.

The weird and wacky

The most evident similarity between the first three films is the use of the surreal, both as a theme and as a style. *Saint Clara* tells the story of a young girl with special powers; she can tell the future and transmit her knowledge telepathically to others. All the adults around Clara are a little odd and eccentric, including her family, her teachers and her friends' parents. The film is replete with apocalyptic and violent scenes and dialogue that is so disjunctive that it resembles a dream. The corridor in Clara's high school is impossibly long, stretching so far that it also resembles a dream or fantasy, and the clothes worn by the characters are predominantly garish and theatrical, in contrast to the bleak Israeli neighbourhood in which the story is set.

Made in Israel, a futurist fantasy about the capture of a fictional character, Egon Schultz, dubbed the world's remaining Nazi, does not concern itself per say with the supernatural, but it likewise employs surreal imagery and organizes scenes in a disjointed and oneiric fashion. Schultz has been hiding in Syria for most of his life, but after an Israel-Syria peace deal is brokered, Syria hands him over to the Israeli authorities to be sentenced in Jerusalem. Whilst in captivity, Danny Hoffman, a rich Israeli businessman, whose own father survived the camps, hires some hit men to kidnap Schultz so that Hoffman (accompanied by his young yet trigger-happy daughter) can personally execute him.

The characters in *Made in Israel* are exaggerated and grotesque; even the putative romantic trumpeter discards all morals when offered the two million dollar bounty promised by Hoffman in exchange for the kidnapping of Schultz. Nevertheless, not unlike *Saint Clara*, there are strong elements of emotion, both tender and violent. This tension is clearly manifest in the treatment of Schultz, who, though in captivity for his horrific past, has to be looked after and fed and kept safe until the trial. Anecdotally, Folman has said in an interview that during the making of the film, the cast was overwhelmed with conflicting feelings for Jürgen Holtz, the well-known German actor that played Schultz. Folman describes in the interview how he was obliged to remind his cast that Holtz had only been born in 1932 and was thus exempt from suspicion or mistrust.

With regard to the world of dreams represented in *Made in Israel*, there is a touch of David Lynch's surreal American TV drama *Twin Peaks* in the film. In one scene the Israeli officer takes Schultz for a meal in an American diner, seemingly in the middle of nowhere; however, it transpires that the diner is not in the middle of nowhere, but is situated upon a piece of US- controlled land near the Israeli-Syrian border. Initially, the owner, donning a white apron emblazoned with the US flag and the 'The Americans' written on it, refuses to serve Schultz and says to the officer (in English, with a thick Israeli accent): 'This is America. We serve no Nazis in America. So if you don't take your fucking Nazi out of here we'll fuck him like we fucked them in Normandy.'[5] However, after the officer convinces him that even Nazis have to eat, the owner agrees to make Schultz a nauseatingly huge American meal comprising of a double cheese burger with two eggs on top with bacon and sausage, fries with mayonnaise and a large coke with ice, which Schultz promptly gobbles up whilst the officer watches.

The Shoah and its effect on modern day Israel

Made in Israel is openly concerned with the role of Holocaust memory within contemporary Israeli society; more specifically, it is interested in the idea of Israeli revenge: would an Israeli individual be capable of cruelly treating, or even executing an elderly Nazi? How could this individual avenge the memory of the Jewish Holocaust victim and still respect Israeli law and human rights legislation? Who has the right to execute the last Nazi on earth? How should he be executed? And so on.

The film ends by categorically providing Israel with the moral upper hand: those charged with guarding the last Nazi treat him humanely, and in the final scenes when the last Nazi is to be taken to the top of a snowy mountain and shot, everyone loses their nerve. The rich businessman, who is waiting with his daughter to execute Schultz, realises that she is getting sick from the cold, so he gives up and takes her home. Then, just at the end of the film, when the trumpeter is standing right in front of Schultz with a gun, he can't bring himself to pull the trigger. Finally, Schultz commits suicide, which conveniently achieves justice without implicating Israel in any wrong doing.

In contrast to the explicit theme of the Shoah in *Made in Israel*, Folman's following film, namely *Waltz with Bashir* broaches the subject very discretely. So discretely, it could even be missed. There are in fact only three overt references to the Holocaust. The first two are during Folman's previously mentioned discussion with his friend, Ori Sivan; the third is at the end of the film when the journalist Ron Ben-Yishai describes the Palestinians that survived the massacre as reminiscent of the Jews who had been liberated from the Warsaw Ghetto at the end of the war. Nevertheless, the three references are clearly fundamental to the understanding of the film, a fact reinforced by their very presence within the screenplay. Indeed, Israeli film scholar Ilan Avisar discusses both *Made in Israel* and *Waltz with Bashir* as examples of Holocaust revenge narratives.[6] Whilst I disagree with this assessment, I concede that the two films might have more in common than meets the eye, and that the Shoah is certainly a shared motif. In Chapter Five I analyse the function of the Holocaust in greater detail within the context of Israeli cinema of the early millennium, and the cinema of second-generation film makers such as Folman.

Why *Waltz with Bashir*?

Considering the similarities between Folman's first three feature films it is curious that only *Waltz with Bashir* achieved such international success – naturally the others became better known as a result, but they have garnered comparatively little scholarly criticism. One likely reason for the film's success is that, unlike *Made in Israel*, which ultimately offers Israel the upper moral hand, *Waltz with Bashir* uses the subject of the Holocaust as a means of reflecting upon Israel's treatment of the Palestinians. It is an explicitly self-critical exploration of war and occupation. This is not to say that Folman is positing an anti-Israel stance, but rather his third film openly grapples with the complexities of Jewish identity as comprising both victim and perpetrator. Ever since the creation of the State of Israel, proclaimed in May 1948, the country has attracted its fair share of criticism as well as support. This criticism was initially from outsiders, although this changed after Israel's needless and ill-fated invasion of Lebanon in 1982 – around which the *Waltz with Bashir* plot revolves – dubbed 'Operation Peace for Galilee', and led by Prime Minister Menachem Begin. Begin declared to IDF staff that the invasion was one rooted in national interest rather than absolute identity. This completely undermined Israel's previous self-image as a nation that was forever noble, only fighting when attacked.[7]

This change of heart, which in turn led to much self-reflection and criticism, has been well documented within Israel but perhaps not so much anywhere else. *Waltz with Bashir* is one of the first internationally distributed Israeli films to express regret about the country's involvement in Lebanon, which is possibly a contributing factor to its global success.

Reinforcing this commercial appeal of a contrite and reflexive Israel is a broad range of accessible intertexts, cinematic, literary and musical, that ensure the film's universality. While cultural references in *Saint Clara* and *Made in Israel* are limited to French singer Edith Piaf's famous rendition of 'Non, Je Ne Regrette Rien' (1960) and the adventures of Bonny and Clyde, *Waltz with Bashir* practically pulses with British and American pop hits from the eighties, and dialogues with film and book classics such as satirical war novel *Catch-22* (Joseph Heller, 1961) and Francis Ford Coppola's epic movie *Apocalypse Now* (1979). As we shall see in Chapter Four, these intertexts allow the film to be both specific and general, overtly reflecting upon the 1982 Sabra and Shatila massacres, but also indirectly commenting on other episodes of the twentieth century – Vietnam, Hiroshima, Korea, and of course the Holocaust.

An additional contributing factor to the success of *Waltz with Bashir* is of course Folman's unprecedented use of animation, which functions as a universal language of its own, and gives other more ethnically or politically specific issues in the film such as Lebanon or Palestine or the Holocaust a form that is familiar to everyone. This is reinforced by the animated flashback scenes and the surreal portrayals of the visions and dreams experienced by the various characters in the film. It is probably fair to say that if you took away the dialogue in *Waltz with Bashir* and just left the music and animated images– of interviews with veterans, tanks, bombed out hangars, even a soldier's fantasy of naked women against a background of OMD and Public Image Ltd. – it would be immediately recognizable, and, more crucially, decipherable.

It is of course impossible to say with complete certainty why one film, rather than another, achieves glory and success. In the case of *Waltz with Bashir* I would argue that it is its unusual animated documentary form, combined with mediations on war that are both general and specific that have led to its stellar reception and criticism. Furthermore, the fact that the film demonstrates an awareness of Israel's responsibility to be mindful of its European history and to remember that the bridge from victim to perpetrator is easily crossed is a feature that would appeal to a large audience. That is, Jews were persecuted in Europe for centuries but their dream of a national home in Palestine has been achieved through the establishment of Israel. The Jews are now in a position of strength and it is up to them to behave morally and humanely towards others, in particular the Palestinians whose military and political position is much weaker. Whilst the Israel-Palestine discourse is very specific, the idea of victims becoming perpetrators is universally applicable. Similarly, whilst Israel's anxiety about entering Lebanon in 1982 is limited to a particular date and region, there are plenty of comparable cases, including the United States military intervention in Vietnam in the sixties and seventies.

The remaining five chapters of this book analyse the mechanisms behind these features that I consider to be unique to *Waltz with Bashir*. How is animation used in conjunction with the documentary format? How does the construction of plot manipulate our understanding of events? How is the tension between the general and specific maintained throughout the film? How is the Holocaust narrative employed? In my concluding remarks I sum up all that has been discussed and offer my thoughts concerning the function and significance of Ari Folman's film.

References

1. See Nirit Anderman, '*Waltz with Bashir* earns best documentary award at international film festival', *Haaretz* (2008) AND *Haaretz Service*, 'U.S. Writers' Guild names Israeli war film *Waltz with Bashir* best documentary' (2009).

2. Patricia Aufderheide, *Documentary Film: A Very Short Introduction* (Oxford: Oxford University Press, 2007), p. 3.

3. Ilan Avisar, 'The Holocaust in Israeli Cinema as Conflict between Survival and Morality', in *Israeli Cinema: Identities in Motion*, ed. Miri Talmon and Yaron Peleg (Austin: University of Texas Press, 2011), pp. 159-160.

4. See *Waltz with Bashir* official website.

5. Ari Folman, *Made in Israel* (2001) time code 00:25:52.

6. Ilan Avisar, 'The Holocaust in Israeli Cinema', op. cit. p. 161.

7. I shall discuss this in further detail in Chapter Four.

Chapter Two: How to Define *Waltz with Bashir*: Animated Documentary or Animated Fiction, or Both?

What is this weird film?

Defining *Waltz with Bashir* is no easy feat; for a viewer completely ignorant of the film's context it probably seems like a wacky and psychedelic mediation on post-traumatic stress amongst war veterans ('Call it an adult psycho-documentary combat cartoon and you're halfway there' says Anthony Lane in *The New Yorker*).[1] The film, after all, shows some bearded middle-aged man going around Israel (and abroad), quizzing his friends and colleagues about a recurring vision. In one scene he is even sharing a spliff with a friend as the two try to piece together their fragmented memories; the spliff of course momentarily undermines any hard-hitting historical enquiry that the narrator purports to undertake. For this very same viewer, there is hardly any information given about the geographical setting of *Waltz with Bashir* (Israel and Lebanon), or the players (the Israeli government, Ariel Sharon, Menachem Begin) and the events (the Lebanese elections, the Israeli invasion of Lebanon, the Holocaust) that are so important to the story.

To the viewer with little knowledge of Israel or Israel's history the only signpost that *Waltz with Bashir* is a documentary is its use of interviews, which I will discuss shortly. There are of course countless types of documentary – political, experimental, and historical – but the singular characteristic that unites them all is the explicit contract between film-maker and viewer that the documentary will give an honest representation of somebody's experience of reality.[2] This experience of reality can be shown objectively or subjectively; it can be restricted to a single individual, for instance, a person's feelings about rain, or poetry, but the reality has to be believed as genuine. The contract between film-maker and viewer takes place especially when the film in question is described either by the director, or the distributor, as a documentary, an act that immediately shapes the expectations of the viewer. It is the naming more than anything that distinguishes a narrative fiction from a documentary since fiction can easily simulate documentary conventions and vice versa.

In this sense, the viewer allows themselves to enter the world that is depicted, and treat it as real and informative in some way. This is the case even with the most avant-garde of documentary: in Stan Brakhage's

Mothlight (1963) the viewer is presented with a series of exquisite images shown at such high speed that there is no time to examine them carefully. Nevertheless, the title *Mothlight* tells the viewer that some kind of reality (hidden) about moths will be displayed. The viewer then imposes this knowledge onto the fast-moving spindly and veined shapes and assumes that they are related to moths or moth wings. In fact, Brakhage had placed dead moths between celluloid strips and then printed the images so that he could project them onto a screen. Of course, without the film's title it is highly unlikely that the viewer would identify the insects. The point is, Brakhage created a signpost for the audience, which is why *Mothlight* is defined as documentary, unconventional though it is.

Likewise, *Dhrupad* (Mani Kaul, 1982) is a film composed of different scenes of men and women dancing and singing. Nevertheless, the title tells us that this dancing and singing is related to the ancient Indian musical genre known as Dhrupad. Furthermore, the film contains occasional voiceovers detailing musical traditions in India, as well as instructions about playing given by the musicians as they perform. *Dhrupad* is not an obvious documentary in the manner of *Triumph of the Will* (a Nazi propaganda film by Leni Riefenstahl, 1934) or *Gleaners and I*, a French documentary about modern-day scavenging (Agnès Varda, 2000) or *Super Size Me*, the social experiment in American fast food culture, (Morgan Spurlock, 2004); but it offers an explicit contract to the viewer via the title which is then recognizable in the film itself.

Waltz with Bashir was not initially marketed as a documentary, nor is there an explicit claim to truth in the title. As I mentioned in Chapter One, the original Israeli film poster just says *Waltz with Bashir* whilst the English-language equivalent contains the subheading 'Based on a true story'. 'Based on a true story' sends a clear message that the film is a fiction inspired by real life events. This is obviously not the same as documentary.

In addition, simplistically speaking, the title (*Waltz with Bashir*) does not suggest an obvious argument, or rhetoric (such as David Guggenheim's *An Inconvenient Truth*, 2006) or an apparent point of interest, or category (as in for example Les Blank's very precise *Gap-Toothed Women*, 1987). To be fair, not many documentaries do have such transparent titles but then they have other characteristics (other than marketing) that put forward

Fig 1: Promotional poster for *Waltz with Bashir*

a claim to reality – authoritative voiceover, historical footage, and talking heads – that mark them out as documentaries. It is the ubiquity of these characteristics that has allowed for the parodying of the documentary form as in the 'mockumentaries' *The Spaghetti Tree* (BBC's *Panorama*, 1957) or *This Is Spinal Tap* (Rob Reiner, 1984).

The Spaghetti Tree, broadcast on April Fool Day as a spoof documentary, shows a Swiss family from Ticino harvesting pasta from trees. The film uses conventional and immediately recognizable documentary conventions including: location filming; atmospheric music; the authoritative male voice-over, recourse to science (the reporter explains the unusual crop in relation to an exceptionally early spring and even mentions a parasite that eats the crops); background information (the reporter talks about the life of the spaghetti farmers); and finally, images of couples enjoying the spaghetti in a restaurant. Meanwhile, *This Is Spinal Tap* parodied the rockumentary by using conventions such as the success narrative, and backstage antics contrasting with brilliant stage performances.

More crucially, as I mentioned earlier, many documentaries are defined as such either because of their distributor (non- commercial distributors such as professional organizations, specialist magazines etc) or the film-maker, who views and presents him or herself as a maker of documentary (i.e. Michael Moore), or because of the funding bodies involved (special interest groups, national agencies). This is pertinent with regard to *Waltz with Bashir* which was sponsored by Israel's Channel 8 (also known as

Noga Communications), the country's leading documentary channel. Channel 8, initially the sole sponsor, provided one hundred and twenty thousand dollars but it became evident that Folman needed more money and so secured financing from other sources. Consequently, at least in the beginning, Channel 8 regarded *Waltz with Bashir* as a documentary and Folman would have described it as such when seeking help from them. Of course, by the time the film was finished, at a cost of two million dollars, this might not have been the case. In the credits, it says that *Waltz with Bashir* was made in collaboration with Channel 8 so to anyone paying attention the documentary credentials are there.

Furthermore, *Waltz with Bashir* was also made in collaboration with the New Israeli Foundation for Cinema and TV which was founded in 1993 by the Ministry of Arts to promote film-making in Israel. Whilst this might suggest a built-in bias necessary for securing support it would be impossible to quantify this, especially since Folman also collaborated with Medienboard Berlin-Brandenburg – a funding agency that has supported a wide variety of international films of all genres, both documentary and fiction. In fact, *Waltz with Bashir* was a notably international venture, produced by the Israeli Bridgit Folman Film Gang and the French Les Films D'Ici and coproduced with Arte France and ITVS International.

The variety of funding and distributive bodies involved in Folman's film can be contrasted to those films that explicitly promote themselves as documentary such as Errol Morris's *The Thin Blue Line* (1988) which was funded by the American Corporation for Public Broadcasting and the National Endowment for the Arts, both of which are listed in Nichols' study as classic examples of bodies that are known for funding documentaries of public interest. On the other hand, Patricia Aufderheide points out that theatres and cinemas downplayed the documentary aspect of Morris's film in order to encourage ticket sales.[3]

The question remains: can *Waltz with Bashir* be categorised as a documentary? This is a tricky question and an important one because it is about evidence. If we are to return to our original stipulations about documentary – that it needs to give an honest representation of somebody's experience of reality, whatever that reality may be – then this surely affects our judgement of *Waltz with Bashir*. Folman received funding from Israel's leading documentary channel but he did not publicly market or promote the film as a documentary per say. On the one hand, marketing matters because how a film is promoted affects expectations concerning responsibility; on the other, it doesn't matter because if critics call it a documentary then it is up to them to deal with the implications. This is pertinent in the case of *Waltz with Bashir* which was largely defined as a documentary and consequently praised and lambasted in equal measure. Yoni Goodman, Director of Animation for *Waltz with Bashir*, said in an interview with website *Design Federation* that he and Folman both expected the film to be treated as a left-wing art house movie and confined to a small audience. [4] Folman, he said, just wanted to make an animated film based on his experiences. From the very beginning, therefore (at least according to this interview), the project was perceived as a story, as a narrative of Folman's experiences. In another interview with *Time Out* critic David Jenkins Folman showed a lack of interest in how the film is categorised, although he sees it as an anti-war film:

> I did my thing and that's it. It's an anti-war film. At least I hope it is. Critics, audiences, schools, they can say whatever the hell they like. 'It's documentary. It's drama. It's bullshit.' That's fine. To make the film and then try to categorise it...I don't have to. [5]

On the other hand, *Waltz with Bashir*'s online press book, presumably created soon after the film's release, contains an interview with Folman where he says that he always wanted *Waltz with Bashir* to be an animated documentary rather than an animated fiction film:

> It was always my intention to make an animated documentary. Since I had already made many documentaries before it was a real excitement going for an animated one. I made an experiment in my documentary TV series...Each episode opened with a three-minute animated scene...it worked so well that I knew that a feature length animated documentary would eventually work. [6]

So it seems that the original plans for the film are unknown and recollection of these plans is inconsistent. This is of course crucial to our discussion because it suggests that Folman and Goodman are just riding on what critics have said. They didn't market or promote the film as a documentary but Folman is seemingly relaxed about critics defining it as such. In the press book he says it was meant to be an animated documentary but in *Time Out* he says he doesn't care. What's interesting is that so many critics and scholars assumed it was a documentary without it being marketed as such and this is clearly to do with its form, which I shall discuss shortly.

Who says it's a documentary?

In 2008 *Waltz with Bashir* was awarded best feature-length film by the International Documentary Association and in 2009 it was awarded Best Documentary by the Writers Guild of America.[7] In his essay 'A Soldier's Tale', Ali Jafaar, who concludes with the accolade 'laced with the uncertainty of a bad acid trip', nevertheless begins his argument by suggesting that *Waltz with Bashir* is an 'excoriating autobiographical account of Israel's 1982 invasion of Lebanon'.[8] Similarly, Garrett Stewart argues for psychic realism where the merging of animation and live footage in *Waltz with Bashir* creates 'a document of disavowal'.[9] The word 'document' is crucial as it suggests that the film could be used as historical evidence. Nurit Gertz and Yael Munk say that *Waltz with Bashir* takes 'Israeli guilt one step further' and stands out from other Israeli films that address the Israeli- Palestinian conflict precisely because it depicts the Lebanon war 'as it was experienced by the director'.[10]

Bill Nichols in the second edition to his classic *Introduction to Documentary* describes *Waltz with Bashir* within the context of metaphor.[11] In documentary, the specific image, say, of a rolling tank, is a metaphorical representation of war and sometimes the visual and aural metaphor can provide us with a deeper understanding of war than a written textual equivalent. Animated documentary, he argues, is especially effective at creating powerful representations of an event. *Waltz with Bashir* is 'a striking example' of an animated documentary because it 'gives a rich, embodied feel for what it was like for Ari Folman, the filmmaker, to be complicit with a horrendous massacre...'[12] The idea of giving the audience 'a rich, embodied feel' for an experience is typical of what Nichols describes in his *Introduction to Documentary* as 'performative', a work that stresses the subjective quality of knowledge.[13] This documentary mode:

'...freely mixes the expressive techniques that give texture and density to fiction (point-of-view shots, musical scores, renderings of subjective states of mind, flashbacks and freeze frames etc) with oratorical techniques for addressing the social issues that neither science nor reason can resolve.'[14]

According to this, Nichols might describe *Waltz with Bashir* as an example of this mode, in which case the animation serves to represent Folman's personal experience as a soldier during the First Lebanon War. I would suggest that using the catch-all term of 'subjective' is a bit too easy for this film which also attempts to describe events in the real world from other perspectives, not just Folman's. The point is that Nichols views the animation in the film as a vehicle for the documentary. There is no ambiguity with regards to his definition.

In all instances, the critics give priority to the documentary format, rather than the animation. This assumes a responsibility on the part of Folman for his alleged subject, namely Israel's role in the massacres. This brings about a specific discourse (or point of discussion), which is rich but ends up narrowing the focus to issues such as the effect of trauma on testimonials, or the value of psychiatry in recovering memory loss, or the ethical protocols of interviewing. None of these, to my mind, actually get to the heart of what the film is about.

Ella Shohat, in the postscript of *Israeli Cinema: East/West and the Politics of Representation* mentions *Waltz with Bashir* within the context of documentary and criticises the film for limiting focalisation (viewpoints) to the Israeli soldiers and not extending it to the Palestinians.[15] This criticism reveals expectations normally – though not always – associated with documentary rather than fiction. Furthermore, Jafaar, Stewart and Gertz all suggest that the documentary format is supported by the final live footage scenes, that there is a clear trajectory, or path, from memory, false or otherwise, to the 'real'. This interpretation also limits possible responses to the film because it imposes a specific purpose-filled logic that completely ignores the ambiguity of documentary as animation. Interestingly enough, the first cut of the movie had two other live-action scenes, towards the beginning and the middle but Folman removed them. So the powerful transition from animated to live action wasn't even an original part of the film.

What's 'documentary' about it?

Waltz with Bashir is structured around ten interview scenes, eight of which are presented as conversations or dialogues between the narrator and the interviewee, and two interviewees' monologues in which the narrator is either entirely absent or exists solely as a disembodied voice off-camera. It is undeniably the insertion of these interviews that has led to the film being considered as a documentary, and more specifically, an interactive documentary, one in which there is a clear encounter between the film-maker and the film's participants.[16] Whilst these interviews are frequently juxtaposed with surreal imagery and flashbacks, the film is perceived as a well-meaning quest for truth in documentary form. This quest, namely to remember what Folman was doing on the night of the massacres, is articulated right at the beginning of the film after his nocturnal drink with Boaz. Because a quest has been established the viewer is invited to take the words and comments of the interviewees more seriously than if the film were presented as pure fiction. He or she is also invited to infer congruence between what is happening in front of the camera – for instance, the scene depicting the Israeli soldiers' jovial entry into Lebanon – and historical reality even if this scene is animated. The interactive mode (if that's what it is, and we'll talk about it later) is especially effective in the film because it highlights the supposed effect made by the interviewer upon these individuals, namely trauma and guilt.

Perhaps more crucially, with two exceptions, the interviewees are not actors, but real people (animated, of course) who were involved in some way in the Lebanon War. This distinguishes it from other films dealing with historical events that also revolve around interviews but are performed by actors, such as *Titanic* (James Cameron, 1997), *Capote* (Bennett Miller, 2005) or *The Bling Ring* (Sofia Coppola, 2013).

On the other hand

The film's production notes openly admit that the interviews are not filmed live, but in a sound studio. For instance, the scene in which Ari and Carmi are chatting in a car is actually the two of them sitting on adjacent seats with Carmi holding a toy steering wheel. Moreover, two of the interviewees, Boaz Rein-Buskila and Carmi Canaan, refused to have their faces exposed in the film and they were both acted and dubbed by professional actors. The entire film was based on a screenplay written by Folman after extensive research. This research, which took over a year, resulted in dozens of testimonies about the First Lebanon War though only a handful was chosen for the film. After the screenplay was written, the film was shot in a studio as a 96-minute video film. This was broken down into a storyboard and then into a video board. After this stage, four illustrators produced two thousand individual illustrations based on the story board and the video board which were then animated.

This highly complex process which revolved completely around the screenplay (and the economy of animating the screenplay) undermines the 'on-the-spot' physical encounter between the filmmaker and their subject that is a key feature of interactive documentary. Nichols says of the interactive mode:

> Beginning in the late 1950s the availability of very portable synchronous sound recording equipment made interaction more feasible than it had been...Speech need no longer be reserved for postproduction in a studio, far removed from the lives of those whose images grace the film. The filmmaker need not be only a cinematic, recording eye. He or she might more fully approximate the human sensorium: looking, listening, and speaking as it perceives events.[17]

The spontaneity and present-tenseness of the interactive form whereby the viewer can judge how the filmmaker and subject respond to each other, where they can assess a change or tremble in voice or in pitch vanishes with a screenplay. Folman's original interviews that he conducted prior to writing the screenplay are clearly the ones that the viewer would really like to see. In these original encounters, Carmi and Boaz would have told him that they didn't want to be exposed and Folman would have reassured them. Surely, this is the content that we would want to witness.

In the film's first scene, when Folman is having a beer with Boaz, Folman complains that Boaz called him up in the middle of the night to which Boaz replies: 'Asshole'. 'Don't call me asshole' says Folman, clearly offended. These two lines, which really belong in a fiction film, show how contrived the so-called interview format is. Boaz doesn't spontaneously call Folman an asshole but it's obviously in the screenplay. We have no idea why, whether it's an approximation of a real conversation or whether it's for dramatic effect.

The same is true when Folman visits his friend Ori Sivan. Folman knocks on the door and then suddenly the camera switches and we see him through Sivan's eyes, distorted through the keyhole. Clearly, in a live action documentary the camera wouldn't already be inside Sivan's house and it certainly wouldn't be looking through a keyhole at the same time as Sivan. The camera obviously stands in momentarily for Sivan's perspective. Then Sivan opens the door and looks surprised: 'What's wrong? It's 6:30 in the morning?' Folman replies: 'We all have friends who are lawyers, doctors, therapists...Sometimes that friendship costs them.' Of course, if this is all based on a screenplay then it probably isn't 6:30 in the morning; maybe it is early afternoon or lunchtime. No one knows. The spontaneity of the visit is in fact completely contrived; even if the original meeting was identical there is no way that Folman could have accurately reconstructed every flicker or movement that originally took place.

Fig. 2: Sivan's keyhole view of Folman

This can be contrasted with Errol Morris's 1988 interactive and non-intrusive documentary, *The Thin Blue Line*, which tells the true story of Randall Adams, who was wrongfully imprisoned following the murder of a Texas policeman in 1976. Eventually, we learn that another man, David Harris, was probably guilty but had not been charged because he was a juvenile at the time. In this film, which is based on real life events and features interviews with both Adams and David Ray Harris, the voice and timbre and eye movements of the participants are intrinsic to the film. A screenplay would probably have changed everything. I would even venture to say that if it wasn't for the live action filming we would never believe that Harris could fool so many people. After all, his friends say that he boasted about his crime sprees, police officers confirmed them and we learn that he has a criminal record anyway. If we never actually saw Harris we'd have no doubts about his guilt. But on screen Harris is a baby-faced boy who appears as though butter wouldn't melt in his mouth. At first glance he is sweet and charming. It's only by virtue of his orange prison suit and handcuffs (only revealed at a later stage in the film) that we suspect he is a dangerous individual. These clues make us pay even greater attention to his expression and the way he speaks as we try and figure him out. The psychological oddities of Harris and his split personality (charming though also violent and deadly) would be more difficult to recreate under a prepared screenplay.

Furthermore, any ethical considerations endemic to the interactive form such as the unequal distribution of power between filmmaker and subject are redundant in *Waltz with Bashir* because even though there is a huge discrepancy between the relaxed chats he has with Boaz for instance, and the interrogatory style conversation he has with Dror Harazi, they have all been okayed with those involved.

Paul Atkinson and Simon Cooper have argued in their fascinating article 'Untimely Animations: *Waltz with Bashir* and the Incorporation of Historical Difference' that in view of the devised screenplay the film resembles an expository-style documentary rather than interactive.[18] Referring to Nichols' definition of the former, where interviews serve as testimony to the filmmaker's argument, Atkinson and Cooper show that Folman use of interviews is over-determined and preconceived and are only used to serve Folman's overarching vision. Nearly all of the interviews begin with Folman saying he doesn't remember what he did the night of the Sabra and Shatila massacres. The film functions, like most expository documentaries, as a logical solution to a problem, in this case, the problem of amnesia. The conversations that follow are in response to this. This is especially the case with Folman's friend, Ori Sivan, whose function is to explain Folman's amnesia, and post-trauma expert, Professor Zahava Solomon who has an identical function. Therefore:

This tight rule of exposition implies that the protagonist Ari Folman always knows what he does not know, for most dialogues are structured around the absent object of his memory and there is a predetermined acceptance of traumatic foreclosure in the plot. The traumatic event does not erupt unexpectedly, in an untimely fashion, but is rather fashioned as a space to be filled in the denouement. [19]

Also, since Folman's amnesia has a very pre-mediated feel – he does, after all get over it, and he had to get over it in order to make the film – the trauma that caused it cannot be seen as the root of the film. It is, argue Atkinson and Cooper a storytelling device, a trope that propels the narrative forward.[20] Thus, when *Waltz with Bashir* shows a confused Folman, it is really showing Folman pretending to be confused, which again completely weakens the idea of a spontaneous encounter and certainly challenges the assumption that trauma is the key to understanding the film. It also challenges the 'documentary' element of the film. Documentary is supposed to offer an authentic view of someone's experience of reality and *Waltz with Bashir* was praised as a documentary that depicted the trauma of the director and his involvement with a chilling massacre. Even if Folman's initial trauma-induced amnesia and subsequent recall were painful, they happened so long ago and their details have been artificially reformed as screenplay.

How about the animation?

To complicate matters of naming and categorizing, *Waltz with Bashir* (bar the final scene) is entirely animated, which is still pretty rare in documentaries. Normally, animation is used in documentaries to showcase something that can't ordinarily be seen, for representational purposes. The first known (though only partially) animated documentary is Windsor McCay's *The Sinking of the Lusitania* (1918) which explicitly tells the viewer of its pedagogic intentions through textual inserts and a narrator. Likewise John Hubley's *Of Stars and Men* (1964) is an animated film narrated by an authorial male voice (astronomer Dr Harlow Shapley) concerning the nature of the universe, of space and time and where man fits in. A later example is Chris Landreth's *Ryan* (2004), a visually grotesque though captivating film about the Canadian animator Ryan Larkin. The film begins with an animated version of Landreth, the film-maker, introducing his subject matter. This, he tells us, is a film about Ryan. There is no ambiguity; the series of animated interviews that follow, even though peopled by characters with large chunks of their heads missing and Henry Moore holes in their hands, describe Larkin's life as an animator. The animation in the film is self-referential and reflexive and serves to describe the mechanics of drawing to the audience.

Waltz with Bashir is not pedagogic and makes no overt claim to sharing a truth that might be useful to the public such as the composition of matter, or how to draw. But it does use animation as a means of representing that which is normally harder to represent with live actors, namely the fantasies, visions and nightmares described by the various characters in the film. The animation in this sense therefore has a 'penetrative' function, meaning it permits us to enter into the minds of the protagonists. Of course this might make more sense if it were only the fantasy scenes that were animated rather than the entire film. If this were the case, then the animation would stand out as serving a clear purpose that would otherwise be impossible for a live film or video recorder to achieve, namely portraying something that does not exist independently of the camera. But *Waltz with Bashir* is odd because it is entirely animated.

You could argue, and I discuss this in further detail in Chapter Four, that the animation also creates a distancing device so that the nightmares and visions neither impact the viewer too much, nor seem too absurd. Much has been written about the distancing function of animation in *Waltz with Bashir* mainly because so many critics have seen the film has an expression of trauma and traumatic events. The animated image implies reality without imposing this reality directly upon the viewer. For some this is a matter of practicality, i.e. no one wants to actually endure blood and gore and murder; for others it is a mark of respect, that is, the animation acknowledges that some things are simply beyond representation.

One example, a scene that is potentially both ridiculous and horrific, is the one in which Folman's friend Carmi Canaan recalls being on an army ship and passing out on deck and hallucinating: in this hallucination he is floating away from a burning ship on a large inflatable naked woman who is both a maternal lifeboat and an object of eroticism. In his hallucination he is saved but his entire crew is suddenly bombed by an overhead warplane. The animation allows the viewer to accept this bizarre image of the inflatable woman, but also allows the viewer to maintain a distance from a troubling and potentially traumatic scene in which Carmi falls into a trance and imagines that his comrades are being burned alive. The animation also constitutes an understanding that the soldier in question suffered great trauma whilst serving. Unfortunately for the viewer, Carmi's vision blocks out what was really happening on the ship; so we share his lapse of consciousness (as part of the entertainment process of the film) and avoid the actual events.

The fact that animation is used to represent almost everything – dreams, flashbacks and 'live' interviews – and everyone, including Folman himself, is of particular interest. First, it underscores the fictive qualities of the documentary genre: the more realistic the conversations and interviews appear, the gestures, the settings, the language, the more one wonders why animation is used at all, thus calling into question the realist motives of the film.[21]

Second, it also suggests a distance between Folman, the director, and Folman, the represented cartoon character, and further undermines the function of the documentary as a representation of the relationship between film maker and subject. In other words, if *Waltz with Bashir* is supposed to be a film by Folman about Folman, then why does he use animation?

Third, unlike live-action documentary where a testimony is mediated by the camera alone, the construction necessary in animation highlights its purely subjective character. In live-action filming the room where the witness is sitting might be rearranged or decorated but the light and play of shadow and the objects themselves cannot be totally controlled by the camera. There is always an incidental element to take into consideration in live recording. You can move a blue chair to the left or to the right and film it from different angles but it will always be a three dimensional object with a particular weight and density. In animation everything is determined by the artist's pen (or, in the case of this film, Flash software). If you want shadow you have to draw it, if you want contrast of light you have to draw it and so on.

This holds true with people; when Folman initially interviewed his subjects, presumably away from a camera, they would have discussed their feelings about Lebanon and about Folman's film. Then when they had to act out a screenplay they would have moulded themselves accordingly. Folman is the only one who would have really seen their expressions, their facial twitches etc. By the time they were recreated in animated form it is possible that all authenticity had vanished. The question you might ask is: is it really possible for an animator to capture someone's exact expression? Or does the animator draw what he or she interprets from the original image? At the beginning of *Waltz with Bashir* when Folman first visits Carmi in Holland he asks if he can sketch Carmi's son and Carmi says: 'Draw as much as you like … it's fine as long as you draw, but don't film.' Although this suggests that Carmi does think that animation is less revealing or honest (and remember he was played by an actor) when we see his son in the snow playing with a toy gun the impact is still powerful. Is this what Folman is trying to prove? Even though an animated image of a generic boy playing at war does not implicate the individual, it does act as a powerful metaphor for war, which is what Nichols alluded to earlier. There is clearly no way of knowing and the film also declines to offer an answer.

What's more, in a straightforward live-action documentary the narration or testimony is either accompanied by live footage or photographs, or it is re-enacted by actors. The paradox in *Waltz with Bashir* is that most of it is represented as 'live' but in cartoon form. Consequently, in *Waltz with Bashir*, whenever an interviewee describes an event, a memory, or a dream it is translated immediately into a particular and highly stylised image so that in spite of the wide range of voices and opinions, there nevertheless exists a visual flatness and conformity.

Atkinson and Cooper discuss this visual flatness with relation to the representation of time and history: the uniformity of the animation brings together all the disparate elements of the film, the past, the present, the dreamt, close ups, aerial shots and presents them as a whole.[22] This is partly to do with the mechanism of animation: the complicated process of animating drawings (and then using computer software) means that there is a large temporal gap between the event represented and its animated form. This is in contrast to filmed footage where the process of filming takes place at the same time as the event. Atkinson and Cooper say that there is therefore a 'presentness' in the manufactured animated image and in the case of *Waltz with Bashir* this 'presentness' eradicates all historical difference so that there is no difference between the description of an event and its re-enactment.[23] Interestingly, Atkinson and Cooper point out, many people have incorrectly assumed that *Waltz with Bashir* was made using rotoscoping where you trace over live-action recording. This is probably because it is assumed that there is a strong link in the film between the events themselves and the representations of these events.[24]

Because the 'presentness' of the animation creates a visual whole the viewer watches it without paying too much attention to see the discrepancy between what one character describes and its visual representation. This is unlike for example *The Thin Blue Line* where the re-enactment of a witness's car driving past the scene of the crime is a source of fascination for anyone watching – details such as which seat the murderer was sitting in or from which side of the road the witness was watching are considered when watching the re-enactments. In this sense *Waltz with Bashir* is more like a fiction film where the viewer watches a series of events or time frames seamlessly without being alerted to shifts between the historical present and past, or shifts between archival footage and present day interviews.

It's not just that the animation creates a unity that erases numerous differences within the film (past, present, dream, reality,) but it also creates a particular external rhythm that exists separately from anything depicted. This is partly to do with the Max Richter score which seems to guide the film along a particular path but also the animation itself. All the characters move in a similarly gliding way, like waves, often gazing pensively into some unknown distance. As Cooper and Atkinson stress this is true of all elements in the film:

> The animation is often unable to register the impact of one person or thing upon another, hence characters walk along a road as if they were floating slightly above the ground in a way that is comparable to their movement in the dream sequences. Whether a character is walking in an airport, being fired upon in a combat situation, or being rounded up to be executed, the pace of movement remains the same.[25]

The question still remains: if this is all true then is *Waltz with Bashir* still a documentary? It is not really an interactive documentary because the encounter between the film-maker and his subjects is completely contrived and determined by a screenplay. I discussed earlier that the film's use of interviews resembles that of an expository mode of documentary because these interviews serve to advance Folman's argument, namely a demonstration of his quest to learn more about his role in Lebanon. It is of course only a demonstration because Folman had already remembered everything before making the actual film.

So what is the function of the film's form?

In this chapter we have thought about how to best define *Waltz with Bashir*; we have established that though it was never marketed or promoted as a documentary it has been critically interpreted as one. Although the expectations of a documentary require responsibility on the part of the film-maker, towards his subject, and towards his audience, Folman has not refuted the definition. *Waltz with Bashir* clearly has characteristics associated with the documentary form, in particular the extensive use of interviews. Although these interviews appear at first glance to be spontaneous and on the spot –late night meetings in bars, impromptu house calls– they are in fact carefully directed according to a screenplay. The interviews do not reveal surprising information because Folman is always aware of what he doesn't know.

As I have already suggested, the really exciting and revealing interviews happened off-screen when Folman went round asking his friends to participate in the film. In this off-screen parallel movie we would see Folman telling Carmi and Boaz and the others about his plan to make a film. He would ask their permission. We would have seen Carmi refuse; maybe Folman was the one to convince him by saying that an actor could be used instead. We might have seen other ex-soldiers saying that they would never, ever take part. After all, we know from the film's production notes that Folman gathered dozens of testimonies yet only used a handful.

Furthermore, what's so weird about *Waltz with Bashir* is that Folman is so blank. If documentaries are supposed to show someone's experience of reality then perhaps it is more a documentary about Carmi and Boaz and Frenkel and Harazi. While we see Frenkel waltzing amongst bullets and Boaz shooting dogs and Harazi hiding on a beach the flashbacks with Folman – bar one or two –just show him walking in a daze. Even in the 'present-day' interview scenes he appears to have no personality. Yet when you watch any publicity interview with him he is wry and chatty and full of enthusiasm about his work. Surely, when carrying out the initial research for *Waltz with Bashir* and trying to overcome his amnesia this was the Folman that took part, not the wooden one we see in the final product. In this sense, if *Waltz with Bashir* is a documentary then it is a dishonest one.

To sum up, I would argue that *Waltz with Bashir* has elements akin to documentary but that it is more a work of fiction. The point is that the choice of form – interviews and flashbacks – and the critical response to the film are themselves extremely revealing. In the following chapter I shall look at how the film's form is further complicated by its narrative structure.

References

1. Anthony Lane, 'Private Wars: *Valkyrie* and *Waltz with Bashir*', *The New Yorker* (2009)

2. Patricia Aufderheide, *Documentary: A Very Short Introduction* (Oxford: Oxford University Press, 2007), p. 3.
    Aufderheide, Ibid. p. 3.
    Aufderheide, Ibid. pp. 13-14.

3. Aufderheide, Ibid. p. 3.

4. Craig Bourke, 'Interview with Yoni Goodman', *Design Federation* (2008).

5. David Jenkins, 'Director Ari Folman on Waltz with Bashir', *Time Out* (2008).

6. Cannes Festival Online Press Book, accessed at www. Festival-cannes.fr.

7. Haaretz Service, 'U.S. Writers Guild names Israeli war film 'Waltz with Bashir' best documentary,' *Haaretz*, February 8, 2009, http://www.haaretz.com/news/u-s-writers-guild-names-israeli-war-film-waltz-with-bashir-best-documentary-1.269661 (accessed February 27, 2011) and Nirit Anderman, ''Waltz with Bashir' earns best documentary award at international film festival,' *Haaretz*, December 8, 2008, http://www.haaretz.com/print-edition/news/waltz-with-bashir-earns-best-documentary-award-at-international-film-festival-1.259040 (accessed February 27, 2011).

8. Ali Jafaar, 'A Soldier's Tale,' *Sight & Sound*, December 8, 2008, 28–31 (28).

9. Garrett Stewart, 'Screen Memory in *Waltz with Bashir*,' *Film Quarterly* 63.3 (2010): 58–62 (62).

10. Nurit Gertz and Yael Munk, 'Israeli Cinema Engaging the Conflict,' in *Film in the Middle East and North Africa: Creative Dissidence*, ed. Josef Gugler (Austin: University of Texas Press, 2011), 164.

11. Nichols, *Introduction to Documentary* (Bloomington: Indiana University Press, 2001), p. 110.

12. Nichols, Ibid. p. 111.

13. Nichols, Ibid., pp. 130-137.

14. Nichols, Ibid., p. 134.

15. Ella Shohat, *Israeli Cinema: East/West and the Politics of Representation* (London: I.B. Tauris, 2010), 286.

16. Bill Nichols, *Representing Reality: Issues and Concepts in Documentary* (Bloomington: Indiana University Press, 1991), pp. 44–56.

17. Nichols, *Representing Reality*, op. cit., p. 44.

18. Paul Atkinson and Simon Cooper, 'Untimely Narrations: *Waltz with Bashir* and the Incorporation of Historical Difference', *Screening the Past* 34 (2012) p. 4.

19. Paul Atkinson and Simon Cooper, ibid. p. 4.

20. Atkinson and Cooper, ibid., p.4.

21. Paul Wells describes this kind of animation as 'animation with documentary tendency', Wells, *Understanding Animation*, pp. 27–28.

22. Atkinson and Cooper, op. cit., p. 14.

23. Atkinson and Cooper, ibid., p. 2.

24. Atkinson and Cooper, ibid., p. 10.

25. Atkinson and Cooper, ibid. p. 16.

Chapter Three: Narrative Structure

This chapter examines narrative structure and its function in *Waltz with Bashir*. More specifically, the chapter examines the interplay of story and plot and draws upon the paradigm outlined by David Bordwell and Kristin Thompson in *Film Art: an Introduction*.[1] A narrative is a sequence of events determined by causality, time and space. Put simply, without knowing when or where or why something has happened, it is difficult to connect a chain of events and understand them as a whole.

In a film, some events within the chain's narrative might not necessarily be explicit. In this case the viewer will have to infer them. Bordwell and Thompson's classic example comes from the opening scene in Alfred Hitchcock's *North by Northwest* (1959).[2] The main protagonist, Roger Thornhill, is leaving an elevator whilst dictating to his secretary. From this we can assume that he has been dictating to her beforehand in his office and he is continuing now. We never see them in his office, we just infer the event. The narrative is already then divided into events that are presented to us explicitly and events that we can only assume take place. The distinction is that between 'story' and 'plot'. 'Story' refers to all events in a narrative, explicit, implicit and inferred. The 'plot' constitutes those events that are visibly and audibly presented to us in the film. The total narrative universe, including both plot and story is called diegesis. If something happens that is not part of the world as depicted in the film, for instance, music played during the opening credits then we call this non-diegetic.[3]

The way in which the plot reveals the story affects our understanding of cause and effect, and therefore affects our understanding of the narrative. In a murder mystery, the story would be: a) murder, b) discovery of body, c) investigation then d) solution. But the plot usually begins with b) the discovery of the body, so we have the effect but not the cause. The solution (d.) will normally reveal the cause, but this only comes at the end of the plot.

There are numerous examples to illustrate the story/plot distinction and its affect upon narrative, but a classic example, given by Bordwell and Thompson, is Orson Welles' *Citizen Kane* (1941).[4] *Citizen Kane* begins with a newsreel announcing Kane's death. That is, the film's plot begins with this announcement. However, the story of Kane is revealed throughout the film and consists of Kane's childhood, adulthood and old age. In other words, the plot begins with the death of the protagonist, and only gradually discloses the protagonist's story as the film progresses. Since the newsreel at the start of the film gives a resumé of Kane's life the viewer learns straight away of Kane's divorces, his failed political career and other such events. Armed with this knowledge, the viewer then watches the rest of the film expecting these things to occur. This creates suspense because although the viewer knows, for example, that Kane's second wife will leave him, or that he will end up alone in a big house, we don't how these things happen. The sequence of cause and effect, our narrative, is thus manipulated by the way in which information is revealed to us.

It is clear that the plot of *Waltz with Bashir*, set out on pages 53-56, is extremely complex, especially from a chronological point of view. It contains nineteen flashbacks. These flashbacks probably constitute more of the film than the other scenes and therefore the viewer is more likely to remember them than anything else. But before analysing the plot let us think about the story, i.e. the actual order and frequency and duration of events as they really happened rather than how they are visibly or audibly presented. This would probably look something like the following:

1. Folman's father experienced the Second World War in some capacity. (Note that we are always talking about the protagonist Folman, as represented in the film, rather than the notional 'real' Folman who directed *Waltz with Bashir*. Therefore, all references to Folman in this chapter refer to the represented character).

2. Folman was ten years old during the 1973 Yom Kippur War (which started after a coalition of Arab states attacked Israel on the holiest day of the Jewish calendar)

3. In 1982, when Folman was nineteen, he joined the army.

4. September 1982: Folman was nearby when the Sabra and Shatila massacres took place.

5. In 2006 (after his meeting with Boaz) he started investigating his role during the massacre.

6. He finally remembered everything.

7. He made *Waltz with Bashir* (inferred).

When comparing the two versions of events, story and plot, we can see that the plot focuses primarily on phase five of the story, namely the investigation part. The film actually begins with Boaz's dream, as it is described in the late night drinks meeting between Boaz and the protagonist, Folman, in 2006. So we can already see that there is a clear discrepancy between the plot's chronology and that of the story. This discrepancy raises questions that I hope to address in this chapter: why is the story plotted like this? Why does the film not recount events in the same order as the story? Why is it significant that the film begins with the investigation?

Let us now begin to answer some of these questions. The story arc covers the life of the Folman character from aged ten (in 1973) to 2006, when he was forty three, a period of thirty three years. Beyond Folman's biography the story arc also reaches back to the Second World War. This creates a total time span of approximately sixty years. The temporal relationship of events in the story is, for the most part, quite evenly spaced. Phases three and four (Folman joins army, and Folman is nearby when massacres take place) are very close in time, as are five, six, and seven (Folman begins investigating; Folman remembers what happened; he makes the film).

Fig. 3: The earliest event on the story arc: Folman's father on leave during the Second World War

To sum up: the story arc covers an evenly spaced period of about thirty years of Folman's life, and about sixty altogether, counting his father's experiences. The screen time (i.e. film's duration) is eighty seven minutes.

Meanwhile, the plot timeline focuses primarily on 2006 – the time of the investigation – and also returns frequently to 1982 during each flashback. We can therefore summarise that the eighty seven minutes of screen time revolve around two periods: 2006 and 1982. Or, to put it differently, eighty seven minutes of screen time skips about fifty years of story time. To confuse matters, the flashbacks that constitute most of the film hardly ever deal with the Folman character, but are mostly traumatic episodes in the lives of the interviewees. The fact that the testimonies of these interviewees cannot be verified makes it even harder to piece together a narrative.

The other events from the story arc (he was ten during the Yom Kippur War; he made *Waltz with Bashir*) are either compressed, as in the former, or simply inferred, as in the latter. Interestingly, the Sabra and Shatila massacre, which as we know, took place in Beirut in 1982 over a period of three days, only comprises a few fragmented scenes in the film's actual plot. The famous live footage at the end of *Waltz with Bashir* shows only the aftermath of the massacre.

It is therefore clear that our understanding of story events is affected by how they are presented in the plot. As I said before, there are nineteen flashbacks altogether in *Waltz with Bashir*, three of which are repeated. Each flashback, except perhaps numbers 8 and 17, is an expression of trauma and portrays the subject participating in an event that he finds upsetting. It is therefore fair to say that the viewer's experience of *Waltz with Bashir* will centre primarily on disturbing scenes of war.

The nineteen flashbacks are not coherently related: for instance, one is Carmi on a boat, one is Ronny driving a tank, one is Frenkel shooting a boy, but they rarely mention each other. Temporally speaking they have no obvious link. There are two exceptions: first, Frenkel insists that Folman was with him the whole time; second, Folman tells Carmi that the latter appears in his vision of the soldiers coming out of the water. Carmi denies this possibility thus confusing any sense of reliability in Folman's vision. As we shall see later, this confusion is compounded when Sivan suggests that Folman's vision is symbolic rather than literal.

From a narrative point of view, the interviewees' flashbacks are interesting because they serve to justify the present tense of the film. For instance, when Folman first visits Carmi in Holland we learn that Carmi is rich and has earned his fortune by selling falafel. Since Carmi doesn't seem to be a particularly cheerful person, the viewer senses that something is wrong. Finally Folman says:

'Everyone thought you'd become a nuclear physicist...they thought that, by the age of forty, you'd be nominated for a Nobel Prize...'

Carmi replies cryptically:

'By twenty, that future was over.'

These comments create suspense: what happened to Carmi? Why is he a falafel king, freezing his backside in snowy Holland, when he could be a successful scientist in Israel or even California? Since the mysterious comments take place just before Carmi's flashback sequences, there appears to be a causal link: Carmi's trauma as a young soldier in Beirut made him escape to the wintry plains of Europe (in light of the Holocaust context, this of course seems ironic). The narrative line in Carmi's story therefore seems to be an open and shut case.

The same cannot be said of all the interviewees. Ronny Dayag, who first appears as a stern-faced man in an office, narrates his flashback to an unseen camera, rather than in conversation with Folman. The office looks ordinary except for two barely noticeable scientific-looking flasks to the left of the screen. There is a child's drawing of a house from which we infer that Dayag is perhaps a family man. There are also a number of milk cartons on the shelf nearby suggesting that he works for a dairy company. We then learn from Dayag's flashback that he was a mummy's boy who miraculously escaped death, whilst his comrades did not and for this he felt guilty. Dayag states clearly that he broke off contact with the comrades' family, because he felt ashamed that he hadn't done more to help his unit and he wanted to forget. The flashback suggests that Dayag behaved weakly. However, the film doesn't tell us what Dayag is doing now (we think he is a father) and there is no evident connection between his present tense and his flashback. However, the ordinariness of his current circumstances suggests to us that he has managed somehow to put his trauma behind him.

But, on the other hand, we have no idea, if, like Carmi, there were expectations for him to become something in particular, expectations that were then dashed. Perhaps he never wanted to have such an ordinary office; perhaps he wanted to be somewhere completely different. Nor do we have any idea if Dayag's personality or outlook was fundamentally altered by his experiences in Lebanon; it just seems as though there is a large gap between the present-day Dayag and the Dayag from 1982.

Fig. 4: Dayag in his office with children's pictures on one side and Yotveta cartons on the other

In contrast to Dayag's almost wishy-washy demeanour, Shmuel Frenkel first appears on screen in the present tense kicking and punching and performing a martial arts routine, presumably for our benefit. This image fits in with the previous scene – a Folman flashback – where a young Frenkel is preening himself on a beach in Lebanon and applying patchouli oil, so that his comrades will always know where he is. Although the karate chopping Frenkel is tough and muscular, whilst his younger self is more feminine and delicate, both images show him as vain and a bit of a show-off. From a narrative perspective, seeing the adult Frenkel like this also creates suspense: why are we witnessing a karate routine? Is this is his job now? Has he become a discipline junkie? Then we learn that Frenkel still uses patchouli oil and, like Carmi, we have a sense that he is still haunted by his time in the army, which is then verified by another flashback where he remembers spraying a young Arab boy with bullets.

The case of Boaz Rein-Buskila is also interesting. When we first see Boaz, it is in a dream (his own), at the start of the film. But then we see him again, in the bar, talking to Folman over late night drinks. He is unshaven and a little scruffy and we can assume that he suffers from sleep deprivation, caused by his recurring nightmares. Boaz doesn't tell Folman anything else about his life, his work, or his relationships. All we know is that he is troubled and he called Folman late that night to ask him for help. We also learn that Boaz has been suffering from these nightmares for two and a half years. He doesn't say if something triggered them, or if anything changed in his life two and a half years ago.

Fig. 5: Folman and Boaz in a bar late at night

Fig. 6: Folman and Boaz in a bar during the day

Later in the film, Folman and Boaz again meet in a bar (to drink shots) but this time it is during the day and the setting is a little jollier. Boaz is still unshaven but he doesn't seem so forlorn. From this meeting, we learn that Boaz used to be in love with Yaeli, Folman's ex-girlfriend. But again, this is the extent of our knowledge. If we made a judgement about Boaz, based purely upon these two meetings, we could easily infer that his experiences in the Israeli army have turned him into a drifting alcoholic insomniac, who spends his time in bars and rarely shaves.

Compared to the chummy and informal nature of these interviewees, that of Dror Harazi is markedly different. Rather than sitting at home, or in a bar, or in a personalised office, Harazi first appears alone on a chair in a plain room. He is wearing a smart shirt but his hands are clutching the chair's arms as though he is anxious. The walls are dark and gloomy and there is no natural light. No posters, no pictures, no other people, nothing. Harazi is slightly overweight and there is nothing sympathetic about the way he has been presented. This is absolutely crucial because the viewer immediately suspects that something fishy is going on with this testimony. Indeed, this is the only interview that is conducted in true interrogatory form whereby the witness is repeatedly asked to ethically justify his actions. In this particular scene, Folman does not feature as a character within the film but simply as a voice and as an imaginary face that Harazi addresses. Folman is now in 'investigative film-maker' mode rather than 'troubled friend' or 'patient' mode. Indeed, it is at this point that the motivations behind the film become blurred: is the Folman character trying to remember what he was doing at the time of the massacre or is he trying to establish what the Israeli army was doing? As a result, this bad-cop interview seems completely out of synch with the others.

Fig. 7: the first present-day shot we have of Harazi, nervously sitting in a stark room

Harazi's flashback shows him being instructed by the Phalangists to provide cover for them. Since this is the primary cause of Israel's guilt regarding Sabra and Shatila it is perhaps fitting that Harazi should be presented this way. On the other hand, by only treating Harazi like this, Folman is excluding himself (and the other interviewees) from a harsh interrogation.

The point is that showing the present tense Harazi as just an overweight middle-aged guy in an empty room, and then juxtaposing this with his actions in Lebanon, creates the impression that he is just a mindless pawn. Unlike the jerky and insomniac Boaz, or the mournful Carmi, or even the dull office man Dayag, Harazi just sits still as though he claims no agency, as though he is untroubled by the past. Again, as with Boaz, we know nothing else about Harazi. We don't know if he is a family man or if he still lives in Israel. We don't know if he likes bars, or martial arts, or if he has photos of his kids in his office. Dror Harazi in 2006 could be Dror Harazi in any year, any place. All we know is that when he was nineteen, or so, he helped provide cover for the Phalangists.

The final interview with the veteran journalist Ron Ben-Yishai also takes place in a bare room but it nevertheless different to that of Harazi. Folman is completely absent; not only do we not see him but we do not hear him either (he makes one or two brief interjections). Ben-Yishai's testimony is thus a monologue rather than an interview. Moreover, his strikingly confident mannerisms create the impression that he has been given completely free reign to describe events as he chooses, with not the hint of interference from Folman and is by extension excluded from the rigour of historical inquiry. I shall discuss this particular point later in Chapter Five. The crucial point is that when we see Ben-Yishai like this we trust him immediately; he seems to be a figure that one respects and listens to and this colours our perception of his subsequent testimony and flashback.

Ben-Yishai relates how upon hearing of possible massacres in the camps he simply returned home and made dinner for his friends. Whilst at dinner, the regiment commander tells him that a massacre has taken place. Ben-Yishai recalls this episode in a surprisingly casual way:

> He mentioned one or two incidents, saying a family was seen shot [...] we talked about it over dinner later.[5]

RON BEN-YISHAI
רון בן-ישי

Fig. 8: Journalist Ron Ben-Yishai looking confident and charismatic

Then, according to Ben-Yishai's flashback, when Ben-Yishai finally does question Defence Minister Ariel Sharon about the massacres, he patiently waits until the next morning before investigating further. It is notable that the present day Folman never questions Ben-Yishai's slow response to the horrific rumours.

So, let us summarise these flashback examples, by asking: what does the reversal of chronology do to our perception? When we first see Boaz, Carmi, Dayag, Frenkel, Ben-Yishai and Harazi in the present tense of the film, in 2006, we are asked to infer what happened to make them the way they are. Why is Carmi in Holland and why is Frenkel an intimidating karate expert? Why is Harazi just sitting there? Who is he? Why is Ben-Yishai being treated so differently? What's so special about him? Why is Frenkel a tough looking karate expert when only a scene before, Folman remembers him as a fairly effeminate man dabbing himself with perfume? In view of the fact that we know absolutely nothing else about the lives of these interviewees (Carmi is an exception), the reversal of chronology creates an immediate causal chain linking Lebanon to the present. If, for example, by way of contrast, we saw Frenkel's army experience in totality first (preening himself on the beach, using patchouli oil so his comrades could find him, and then killing a young boy) followed by what he is like in the present day; we might wonder about all the years in between: leaving the army, getting a job, getting married, etc. Frenkel may have liked karate even before he joined the army; we just don't know. The juxtaposition of the Frenkel scenes, however, suggests a causal link between trauma and being a fearsome martial arts expert. Similarly, if we had seen the journalist Ben-Yishai's activities and response to rumours first and then the interview, we might be more sceptical about the way his interview has been conducted. We might also wonder about his career following the war and what he had done during the twenty years between Lebanon and the present day.

These internal examples reflect the overall structure of the film which is plotted to emphasise the link between present day Israeli trauma and Israeli army experience during the First Lebanon War. This is why, in spite of the evenly spaced story arc that covers sixty years, the plot only really explores two periods – 2006 and 1982- through the surreal testimonies of a selection of mostly male characters (Professor Zahava Solomon is in fact the only female character to be interviewed). This structure consequently plays down the role of the intervening years for these characters. For instance, if you believe that *Waltz with Bashir* is an authentic documentary that chronicles the life of the 'real' Folman then you might notice that the film never touches upon his successful career in television, or how he went travelling with friends, or anything else. If you knew nothing about the 'real' Ari Folman you would think from this film that he lived on his own, didn't have much of a social life and you would never, ever guess that he was quite a celebrated director in Israel. The desire to emphasise the link between present day Israeli trauma and Israeli army experience also explains why the film is structured almost entirely around flashbacks: flashbacks are simply memories of events, versions of events that have been moulded and shaped by present day circumstances. The viewer cannot be sure if any of the flashbacks are reliable, which means that his or her understanding of the events of 1982 is based upon shaky premises.

The result of all this is that the film appears to be a disjointed sequence, of mostly surreal events. This is especially true of the three repeated flashbacks, which give the impression that time isn't moving at all. Ronny, Carmi and Folman all have flashbacks that contain water sequences but the significance of this is ambiguous. Is it that they were all present? This might seem the most logical guess. However, Folman's friend Sivan suggests that the water in Folman's flashback is purely symbolic:

What does the sea symbolise in dreams? Fear. Feelings. The massacre frightens you, makes you uneasy. You were close to it...[6]

If the sea really does symbolise fear, does this apply to Carmi and Ronny's visions too? Obviously there is no answer but as a result of Sivan's hypothesis there is now a possibility (within the film) that some of these flashbacks exist completely out of time, and simply represent emotions. The main point is that while the story arc makes it clear that Folman's experience of the First Lebanon War constitutes a relatively small part of his life, with relatively little or no contact with the men interviewed, the inverse is true of the plot which centres mainly on the visions and flashbacks of the interviewees. These are then joined by Folman's flashbacks and visions. Together these create the impression that the film is an-out-of-control sequence of events, where one traumatic image follows another leading to the harrowing final scenes of live footage. As we have already established in the previous chapter, this impression is artificial because when Folman made the film, he had already processed his memories, and those of his interviewees.

Let us now look a bit more closely at the relationship between story events and their representation as plot. The earliest event in the story arc (phase one, 'Folman's father experienced the Second World War') is only alluded to briefly in the film, just before flashback nine, and therefore only makes up a tiny part of the plot. Folman is in a bar drinking shots with Boaz Rein-Buskila and reminisces about how his father used to try and comfort him during army service by describing the tough life of a Russian soldier in the forties. On screen we are shown some young (presumably Russian) soldiers getting off a train and kissing their girlfriends before heading back immediately to fight. This seems like quite a trivial reference to the Second World War and you could argue that it retrospectively clashes with Sivan's Holocaust diagnosis that takes place much later in the film.

Sivan's diagnosis, which takes place towards the end of the film, is that Folman has been thinking about the Holocaust from the age of six. Crucially, Sivan is not a professional therapist. Scholars and critics endlessly refer to Sivan as a psychiatrist or a shrink, but this isn't backed by the film itself. Sivan is in fact just a very good friend who likes to come up with helpful ideas.

It is therefore not surprising that his diagnosis is never actually confirmed by Folman himself. In other words, we can't be sure if Folman has been thinking about the Holocaust from aged six because he never agrees or disagrees with Sivan. This is why it is in the plot but not in the story. If you were to add it to the story arc it would be second, but you would have to put a question mark next to it. In other words, if you added it to the story arc, it would be the second earliest event (right after 'Folman's father experienced the Second World War').

Significantly, this reference to the Shoah, which actually appears twice in the plot but can't be verified in the story, is nonetheless presented as one of the most crucial aspects of the entire film. The subject of the Holocaust in *Waltz with Bashir* is presented as the possible basis for the entire investigation and this is reinforced at the end of the film during flashback nineteen when Ben-Yishai evokes the liberation of the Warsaw Ghetto.

Let us examine more carefully the two scenes with Sivan in which the Holocaust is mentioned. The first takes place during Folman's second visit to Sivan (after an hour into the film) and then again eleven minutes later when he pays Sivan a final visit. In the first instance, Ori Sivan, who as we remember is not a qualified shrink, suggests that Folman's amnesia regarding events in Lebanon stems from his preoccupation with the Holocaust and that in order to overcome this amnesia Folman should carry out an investigation based on testimonies from other Israeli soldiers:

> Your interest in those camps is actually about the 'other' camps [...] your only solution is to find out what really happened [...] get details and more details [...].

Although Folman's sole response to this is a bemused smile, the analogy has been made and is firmly embedded both in the text and in the spectator as a possible discourse. Consequently, there is a perpetual and unsettling dialogue between very recent and distant Jewish history. The process of Folman's historical inquiry into the responsibility of those who participated, either wittingly or unwittingly, in the Sabra and Shatila massacres is mediated by another pressing historical investigation, namely that of witnesses – both victims and perpetrators – to the Shoah. The verdict reached via this process is revealed by Sivan towards the end of the film and, inasmuch as Folman does not protest, it remains in the mind of the viewer as viable:

At age 19 you felt guilty – unwillingly you took on the role of the Nazis.

Unsurprisingly, this verdict, which as I said, comes almost at the end of *Waltz with Bashir*, casts each of the previous interviews and conversations in a different light: rather than simply asking individuals to retrace their steps, Folman has also been querying to what extent they are different from those who carried out orders under Nazism. In this sense, a very cursory piece of non-verifiable material given during the plot is transformed into a key to understanding the film. The fact that Sivan is only (amateurishly) speculating that Folman's curiosity is rooted in the Holocaust potentially undermines the importance or value of this key. In any case, there is undoubtedly a clash between what the Folman character chooses to actively discuss and what Sivan thinks he should be discussing. Obviously this clash is artificial because both Second World War references are in the film. The question then is whether this artificial clash has a function. Why is it in the film? I shall discuss the function of the Holocaust in greater depth in Chapter Five.

Fig. 9: Folman's bemused reaction to Sivan's theory

So, let us sum up: the earliest point of Folman's story arc, which is visibly, though briefly, presented in the plot, is that his father experienced the Second World War. This is revealed casually in a bar with an anecdote about only having a few minutes to see your girlfriend, and is arguably trivial in the light of the film as a whole. Meanwhile, the second earliest point of Folman's biography, according to the plot alone, is that Folman has been thinking about the Holocaust and the concentration camps from the age of six. This speculative diagnosis is never confirmed by Folman and so we can't add it to our story arc.

This leads us into the question of causal chains: why did the Folman character carry out his investigation? Why did he make the film? What effect did certain events have on him? The plot arc gives us two contrasting answers. The first is at the start of the film when Boaz and Folman meet for a late night drink. Boaz tells Folman that he called him because Folman is a film-maker and films can be 'therapeutic'. According to this, it is Boaz who has planted the idea of the film into Folman's mind. However, later on in the film, Sivan offers the 'real' reason: Folman is subconsciously drawn to the investigation and the project because deep down, he identifies himself with the Nazis. Although Folman never verifies this diagnosis, the fact that it is in the film indicates that it should be taken seriously.

The two different reasons have implications for how the film should be interpreted: is *Waltz with Bashir* an investigative enquiry into Israel's role in the Sabra and Shatila massacre? Is it an enquiry into how Israel should learn from its own history and take responsibility for its actions? Or, is the film a type of therapy? Is it a way of enabling veterans, such as Boaz, to come to terms with their trauma? There is no clear answer to these questions since the film allows for all possibilities.

So what does the interplay of story and plot tell us about the film?

The plot of *Waltz with Bashir* centres on two time periods, 2006 and 1982. But the story arc covers a period of about thirty years of Folman's life, and about sixty altogether, counting his father's experiences. Meanwhile the film lasts eighty-seven minutes (or one hour and twenty-seven minutes) then eighty-seven minutes of screen time skips about fifty years of story time. On top of that the events of 1982 are mostly told via flashbacks and visions which may or may not be reliable.

The constant juxtaposition of the two time periods, 2006 and 1982, necessarily creates a causal link between them. We see the shaky and nervous Dror Harazi in 2006 and then we assume he is like this because of the subsequent flashback. Similarly, we first see Boaz within his own nightmare in 2006 and again in a bar looking troubled. The subsequent flashbacks with the dogs reduce Boaz to this singular event. We know nothing else about him, or indeed, any of the others.

The way in which the story's events are revealed to us in the plot affects our understanding of these events. From the plot alone we would assume that there was a smooth course beginning with the late night drink and ending with the live footage. We would presume that Folman gathered information very easily and tracked down his former comrades without any problem. We would also assume that his investigation only lasted a week or so. We might imagine that the live footage signalled a new beginning for the Folman character that would be realised off screen. Yet we know from analysing the film and its production that these assumptions and guesses are incorrect. This discrepancy reinforces the fact that the interplay of story and plot has a powerful effect on the spectator and his or her understanding of events.

Plot breakdown

C. Opening credits: black dogs running through street

1. Bar: Boaz Rein-Buskila and Ari Folman having a drink

Flashback 1: Boaz and the dogs.

2. Boaz and Folman say goodbye and Boaz drives away

Flashback 2: Folman's vision: three men emerging from water; they get dressed and see fleeing figures dressed in black.

3. Folman visits friend Ori Sivan who describes an experiment to him

4. Folman visits Carmi Canaan in Holland

Flashback 3: Carmi's experience on boat followed by Israeli massacre of family.

5. Folman tells Carmi about his flashback

Flashback 4: Identical to Flashback 2.

6. Folman leaves in cab and experiences a real memory

Flashback 5: Folman ordered to dump dead bodies.

7. Folman visits Ronny Dayag in his office

Flashback 6: Ronny's escape and reunion with fellow soldiers.

8. Back to an unspecified beach where Israeli soldiers are having a great time and singing 'Today I bombed Sidon.' Folman narrates. He mentions fellow soldier Frenkel who wore Patchouli oil.

9. Interview with Frenkel in gym

Flashback 7: Frenkel kills young Palestinian boy.

10. Folman visits trauma expert Professor Zahava Solomon who talks about a case study involving a soldier who was also in Lebanon in 1982

Flashback 8: Folman's army leave plus childhood memory of 1973.

11. Folman in a bar with Boaz drinking shots

Flashback 9: Folman in Lebanon.

12. Ron Ben-Yishai in a bare room talking to camera

Flashback 10: Ben-Yishai recalls RPG shooting in streets

13. Now Frenkel in a room talking to camera

Flashback 11: Frenkel switches guns with another soldier and then waltz scene.

14. Folman is back in Holland with Carmi sharing a spliff

Flashback 12: Carmi's memory of Bashir.

Flashback 13: Identical to 2 and 4.

15. Folman now with Ori Sivan, who introduces subject of the Holocaust

16. Dror Harazi talking to camera and describing his memories

Flashback 14: Israeli soldiers instructed to provide cover for Phalangists.

17. Now back to Ron Ben-Yishai's testimony

Flashback 15: Ben-Yishai recalls hearing rumours about a massacre

18. Back to Dror Harazi

Flashback 16: Harazi hears shots from within the camp.

19. Back to Ben-Yishai's flashback and recollections

Flashback 17: He calls Defence Minister Arik Sharon to tell him about massacre

20. Folman back with Sivan talking about the massacre

Flashback 18: Folman remembers that he was with the soldiers shooting flares

Flashback 19: Ben-Yishai's description of 'Warsaw Ghetto' image which then merges into Folman's flashback and then becomes live footage.

References

1. David Bordwell and Kristin Thompson (eds.) *Film Art: An Introduction* (Boston: McGraw Hill, 2003)

2. Ibid. p. 70.

3. Ibid. p. 70.

4. Ibid. pp. 91-102.

5. Ari Folman, Waltz with Bashir, time code 01:11:10.

6. Folman, *Waltz*, ibid., time code, 01:02:18
    Folman, *Waltz*, ibid., time code 01: 02:38.
    Ibid. 01:13:52.

Chapter Four: *Waltz with Bashir* and Meditations on War

The subject of war and film is clearly a vast one. Definitions of the war film genre vary. Is a war film one that specifically depicts a particular battle as in *Saving Private Ryan* (Steven Spielberg, 1998)? Or is it one that represents the effect of war upon a particular group or individual, as in *Taxi Driver* (Martin Scorsese, 1976) or *A Mighty Heart* (Michael Winterbottom, 2007)? How about the so-called anti-war films such as *Apocalypse Now* (Francis Ford Coppola, 1979) or *When the Wind Blows* (Jimmy T. Murakami, 1986)? James Chapman suggests in his excellent study *War and Film* that even if a film displays the horrific side of conflict it is nevertheless representing this conflict, and in this sense, it is still a war film.[1]

Chapman proposes three very fluid categories of war films: war as spectacle; war as tragedy, and war as adventure. Films can be any one of these or a combination of the three. Of course you could categorise films in lots of other ways but for the sake of pragmatism these three groups have been chosen. If we were to apply Chapman's criteria then *Waltz with Bashir* would be chiefly a portrayal of war as tragedy. Clearly this is an extremely broad category and contains a multitude of complexities and variations: tragedy for those involved, and tragedy for the perpetrators, who must collectively carry the burden of murder and devastation, and tragedy of course for the defeated.

Waltz with Bashir, as we have seen from the first three chapters, has been discussed within a range of contexts: animation, documentary, and trauma. It has also been discussed within the context of the anti-war film genre (war as tragedy). Chapman defines the anti-war film as one that: '...expresses, through either its content or its form, the idea of war as a moral tragedy and a waste of human lives.'[2]

Ari Folman, inadvertently subscribing to Chapman's quotation, sees *Waltz with Bashir* as an anti-war film. Indeed, he has said that he dedicated *Waltz with Bashir* to all the children that were born during its production, in the hope that in fifteen years' time they will watch it and not understand what's going on and in the hope that it will depict a reality which is totally alien.

Several non-Israeli critics have similarly viewed *Waltz with Bashir* as an anti-war film in the vein of Coppola's *Apocalypse Now*. Michael Sragow, writing for the *Baltimore Sun* in 2009, observed that '*Waltz with Bashir* is an anti-war movie that becomes a genuine odyssey...War registers as a rip in the very fabric of civilisation...'[3] *Rolling Stone's* Peter Travers wrote that the film should be credited for its 'hallucinatory brilliance in the service of understanding the psychic damage of war.'[4] Rene Rodriguez from *The Miami Herald* asserted that *Waltz with Bashir* was 'not only a harrowing anti-war plea' but 'a deeply moving argument that it is critical to never forget human atrocity, lest the past be repeated.'[5] Peter Bradshaw wrote in the *Guardian* that 'Folman might have created his generation's very own *Apocalypse Now*.'[6] In a similar vein, Jonathan Freedland, also for the *Guardian*, wrote that Folman's film will 'surely take its place alongside *The Battle of Algiers* and *Apocalypse Now* as among the very best films about conflict.'[7] In *Newsweek* David Ansen asserted that: 'These depictions of the dementia of war have a hallucinatory power that can stand alongside those of *Apocalypse Now*.'[8] And Jonathan Curiel from the *San Francisco Chronicle* wrote hyperbolically:

> Think of the most mind-boggling scene in a war film – say the one in *Apocalypse Now* where a shirtless Robert Duvall proclaims (as bombs fall and fires rage) 'I love the smell of napalm in the morning'...Now, ratchet that up ten times, and that's what to expect from this juggernaut of a film.[9]

The association with *Apocalypse Now* is a pertinent, not just because of the direct references Folman makes about the film (including his own surfing on the beach scene), but because of the similarities between Israel and America's respective cultural responses to Lebanon and Vietnam. First, unlike the Second World War, which American popular memory has always perceived as the 'good war' – fighting fascism and restoring democracy – perceptions of Vietnam were altogether more ambivalent. Though, initially, US involvement was validated in the eyes of the public by ideological concerns, this changed very quickly and public opinion reflected an increasingly anti-war stance. While very few American films dealt with Vietnam during the time of the conflict, Chapman writes that once it had ended in 1975 this all changed. Indeed, for Hollywood the 1980s became the Vietnam decade.[10] Of course, one of the most well-known of these films is *Apocalypse Now*, released in 1979.

Fig. 10: Folman's surfing on the beach scene

Similarly, Israel's incursion into Lebanon in June, 1982, led by Menachem Begin's right-wing Likud government, marked a fundamental shift in Israel's self-perception. Until 1982 all wars fought by Israel had been deemed absolutely necessary for the country's safety and survival. Not so with the First Lebanon War, which was carried out for political, rather than security reasons. The war was viewed abroad and by the majority of the Israeli public as a war of choice, rather than necessity and as a scandalous failure. This was mostly to do with the large number of Israeli casualties, coupled with the horror of the Sabra and Shatila massacres, as well as the fact that Israel had now become entangled with south Lebanon and would not disentangle itself until 2000, and even that was short lived.[11] Israel's critical response to the Lebanon War also led to the resignation of then Defence Minister, Ariel Sharon, and later the resignation of Prime Minister Begin.

With the exception of *Ricochets* (Eli Cohen, 1986), the Israeli film industry, like Hollywood with Vietnam, was relatively late in responding to the events of 1982. But unlike the rich bounty of Vietnam films there are only a few about the First Lebanon War besides *Waltz with Bashir*: *Cherry Season* (Haim Bouzaglo, 1991); *Cup Final* (Eran Riklis, 1991), and *Lebanon* (Samuel Maoz, 2009). *Beaufort* (Joseph Cedar, 2007) was in fact set during Israel's withdrawal from Lebanon in 2000 though it frequently refers to the events of 1982. [12]

Ricochets, which was made in collaboration with the IDF (Israeli Defence Forces) constitutes a largely patriotic stance towards Israel's role in

Lebanon. This is in spite of the fact that it was unconvincingly marketed as otherwise.[13] The remaining films, *Waltz with Bashir* included, have all been praised as directly critiquing Israel's national narrative (a small and defenceless Israel versus a large mass of nameless Arab enemies) and similarly questioning Israel's actions in Lebanon. A great deal could be said about of each of these films that would discredit such positive reviews but the fact remains that they were widely viewed by the public as 'harshly critical texts about the Israeli establishment' and its part in a supposedly unnecessary conflict.[14] *Waltz with Bashir* was therefore also perceived as an anti-war movie that interrogated the actions of the Israeli government and military and we shall look at this in more detail shortly.

Chapman identifies several common anti-war themes and archetypes present within the Vietnam film cycle – *Apocalypse Now*, in particular – that can also be applied to *Waltz with Bashir*: moral confusion; internal conflict; dissociation from any historical context; and the dynamic between the innocent recruit and the tough commander.[15]

In *Apocalypse Now*, moral confusion relates to both sides: the protagonist, Captain Willard, travels through Vietnam as though in a dream, witnessing American atrocities and bloodshed. But it is not only American violence that we hear about: when Willard finally gets to Colonel Kurtz, the latter relates a horrific episode concerning a particular village in which the Viet Cong chopped off the arms of all US-vaccinated Vietnamese children. Moreover, the cruelty of the Viet Cong is revealed by Kurtz during the latter half of the film in an almost revelatory way, and more problematically, in a way that serves to justify his own actions in Cambodia:

> And then I realised...like I was shot. Like I was shot with a diamond... And I thought my God, the genius of that...The will to do that...And then I realised they were stronger than we. These men...who had children... but they had the strength to do that. If I had ten divisions of those men our troubles here would be over very quickly.[16]

Through the delusional Kurtz, war is presented as the cause of madness and cruelty, but also as the cause of brilliance. As he reminds us, the Viet Cong also had families and children, but war rapidly eroded their conscience, and caused them to carry out barbaric atrocities.

Meanwhile, in Folman's film issues concerning morality relate to two parties: the Israeli establishment (the government, the military) and the Christian Phalangists. Throughout the film we witness arbitrary killings of innocent Palestinian families by Israeli soldiers; at one point Folman visits an empty villa in Lebanon now occupied by the IDF and we see an Israeli commander watching a German porn movie involving a red Mercedes. The commander then tells his soldiers he has received a hot tip and that they should blow up all red Mercedes. Taking into consideration modern European Jewish history, the fact that an Israeli, after watching a German porn film, featuring a German make of car, should do this, is clearly an ironic commentary upon Israeli morality, especially that of its military.

In the opening scene, as we know, Boaz Buskila describes how he was ordered to cold-bloodedly murder all of the dogs in a Palestinian village. Though this act is described in terms of Boaz's trauma, thus obscuring its cruelty, the Israelis are nevertheless implicated in the unnecessary death of innocent animals. The fact that Boaz obeyed, rather than disobeyed his commander and went along with the execution is not discussed. Boaz is represented as a victim of war, as much as the dogs.

However, I would argue that the absolute viciousness of war, as exemplified by the Viet Cong in *Apocalypse Now*, is reserved in Folman's movie for the Christian Phalangists, who, like the Viet Cong are described as nevertheless capable of love, as in Kurtz's claim that those who amputated the inoculated children had families of their own. In a similar tale of mutilation Carmi Canaan explains to Folman that the Sabra and Shatila massacres were to be expected:

> I don't understand why people were so surprised that the Phalangists carried out the massacre. I mean, I always knew how ruthless they were. During the storming of Beirut, we were in the slaughterhouse... the junkyard where they would take all the Palestinians to interrogate them and eventually to execute them...The Phalangists trafficked the body parts of murdered Palestinians preserved in jars of formaldehyde. They had fingers, eyeballs...and always the pictures of Bashir.[17]

Carmi explains further: Bashir was to the Phalangists what David Bowie was to him; they worshipped him; they adored him and so when he was assassinated it was as if their wife or sister had been killed. Naturally, concludes Carmi, in view of this great love and respect, Bashir's death would be thoroughly and ruthlessly avenged. By describing the scene in the 'junkyard', Carmi is insinuating that the Phalangists are by their very nature a cruel people. The Sabra and Shatila massacre was therefore not carried out because of war, and the moral erosion it provokes, but because a cruel group of people felt a perverse love for their assassinated would-be President. Folman's film suggests that while Israel's moral lapses can be explained as an unfortunate by-product of the war zone, those of the Phalangists cannot. When Folman tells his psychiatrist that with regard to the massacres he was in the second or third circle of responsibility he is dissociating himself from the innate cruelty of the first circle to one of necessity (outer circles). The fact that a few scenes earlier, Sivan speculates that Folman is linking the Sabra and Shatila camps to the Auschwitz camps means that this dissociation is especially noteworthy. The Final Solution (Hitler's plan to eradicate the Jewish people) wasn't conceived during a moment of wartime chaos; it was planned thoughtfully and carefully by people who believed it was the right and moral thing to do, because it was in the interest of a new and powerful Germany.

Fig. 11: scene showing ruthless Phalangists, jars of body parts and Bashir poster

Tied up with the notion of moral confusion is the sense of a lack of purpose. In both the cases of Vietnam and Lebanon public outcry was partly due to the feeling that the war was needless and that it lacked a true purpose. Neither Israel nor America really needed to occupy the countries in question, and when both countries incurred terrible losses this fact became harder to stomach. Chapman argues that the oneiric and disjointed narrative in *Apocalypse Now* could be interpreted as a reflection of this lack of purpose.[18] Even Willard's mission seems preposterous: to leave the safety of America, to return to Vietnam, to travel up the Nung River to Cambodia and track down an American renegade. Not surprisingly, Willard's comrades are shocked that the mission involves taking out a US citizen.

In his article, "Mom, I'm Home': Israeli-Lebanon War Films as Inadvertent Preservers of the National narrative', Yuval Benziman points out that a common motif is the soldiers' putative ignorance about why they are fighting.[19] Benziman reads this tendency as an unconscious strategy to criticise the Israeli establishment, whilst also preserving it. That is, the soldiers may participate in the war, and obey their commanders, as with Boaz Rein-Buskila and the twenty-six dogs, but they can also distance themselves from the situation through shame, regret or claims of ignorance.[20]

Waltz with Bashir, which is premised upon an amnesia-induced ignorance, contains several examples of veterans saying that they were also ignorant at the time of fighting. In one notable flashback scene, the young Folman character has been put in charge of a tank. He and the other soldiers are shooting maniacally in all directions. One of the soldiers suddenly panics and asks Folman what to do. Folman replies: 'Shoot'. The soldier says: 'At who?' Folman answers: 'How do I know? Just shoot.' The soldier then says: 'Isn't it better to pray?' Folman snaps back: 'Then pray and shoot.'[21] The young Folman doesn't even know what or whom he is supposed to be shooting. In this scene a lack of purpose is interwoven with moral chaos; first you ask for God's help, perhaps His forgiveness, and then you shoot at anyone and anything.

Chapman identifies internal conflict as a further marker of anti-war cinema and he cites *Platoon* (Oliver Stone, 1986) which centres on mistrust and bullying amongst American soldiers, as the most schematic example.[22] Similarly, in *Apocalypse Now*, the entire plot is based upon internal distrust: Willard has been given a top secret mission to take out a fellow American (Kurtz) and he's not allowed to tell anyone, even his comrades, who risk their lives to accompany him. When Willard eventually reaches Kurtz the latter is seen to be leading a primitive and barbaric existence; everywhere Willard looks there are corpses swinging from trees; skulls poised on rocks, makeshift cages for dissenters and at the centre a seemingly insane Kurtz spouting bits of philosophy and literature. Even though Willard concedes that he understands Kurtz's views, however unpalatable they may be, he ends up following orders and killing him. Thus the film's ultimate act of violence centres on two Americans. Willard's act of killing ensures that, like Boaz in *Waltz with Bashir*, the film critiques the establishment (in this case the US army) and yet preserves it. The fact that Willard goes through the process of trying to understand his target, of trying to empathise with him makes him seem thoughtful but tormented. After he leaves Kurtz's compound there is a sense that Willard has done his very best in spite of the difficult circumstances and that he has murdered Kurtz only after much soul-searching. Even more problematic is that Willard believes that Kurtz wants to be killed, to have the pain taken away. Willard is saving Kurtz, he is relieving him of his misery. With this in mind, Willard's final act is portrayed as a moral and noble one.

The theme of internal conflict is more ambiguous in *Waltz with Bashir*. On the one hand, when Folman meets up with his interview subjects there is very little warmth or affection, even with the ones who are nominally Folman's friends, and who enjoy relaxed interview settings such as Carmi, in a living room, or Boaz in a bar. Carmi even seems slightly harassed by all the questions. The three men seem quite awkward together even though they are supposedly former comrades. And Carmi, Folman and Boaz seem to have no recollection of their service together; only Frenkel, who isn't interviewed in a 'friendly' setting, reassures Folman with some measure of enthusiasm that were together during the army. Meanwhile, Ronny Dayag tells Folman that he felt so ashamed for having survived his fellow soldiers that he broke off all contact with their families after the war. On the face of it, *Waltz with Bashir* paints a very fragmented picture of the Israeli military experience.

Perhaps the most individualistic scene in the film is during the infamous 'waltz.' During a round of heavy gunfire the young Frenkel realises that he can't shoot with a Galil and wants to change to a MAG, so he asks a fellow soldier, Erez, if they can swap. Erez tells him to shut up and leave him alone because the situation is too dangerous to worry about changing guns. Instead of respecting Erez's (logical) wishes Frenkel decides to threaten him and get the MAG by sheer force. Even though Erez would now be at risk, shooting with an unfamiliar Galil, Frenkel doesn't care and runs across the street. At this point the so-called waltz scene begins. It is fitting that Frenkel's selfish behaviour is followed up by this scene in which he seems to be dancing on his own, to a dance associated with couples. The implication is that he is dancing with Bashir, whose poster can be seen just above Frenkel's head. A further implication is that Frenkel has reneged on his duty towards his fellow soldiers and is now 'dancing' with Bashir and by default, the Phalangists.

On the other hand, the fact that Folman and his interviewees are all able to get back in contact with each other after twenty years apart implies an unspoken fraternity. [23] There is even a sense of unity in their shared amnesia, as if they all belong to the same PTSD support group. Although Carmi appears mildly put out by Folman's investigation everyone else is willing to cooperate even when it places them in a negative light, as with Dror Harazi. And if we assume that Folman began the investigation partly because of Boaz's plea for help – the film begins with Folman responding to Boaz's late night phone call – then this similarly reinforces the feeling of a brotherhood. Therefore, on the surface, *Waltz with Bashir* depicts internal conflict, both from the present day and the past; a deeper reading reveals that the soldiers' bond is actually intact after two decades, a fact proven by the success of the interviews. The level of cooperation amongst the veterans actually glorifies the army and its ethos of a brotherhood.

Chapman identifies dissociation from historical context as a key characteristic of anti-war cinema: 'What the films evoke is the atmosphere of war – its boredom, exhaustion, futility, and horror...'[24] Again, *Platoon* is an ideal example of this: so much of the film portrays the soldiers just hanging out, either getting high on opium or playing cards or drinking beer and getting into fights. There is absolutely no sense of historical context; the Vietnamese, described only as gooks, are either cowering in a village or darting menacingly through the jungle, partially glimpsed, camouflaged by leaves. We have no sense of why they are out to get the Americans, and vice versa. The conflict between the Americans and the Vietnamese does not constitute the main drama of the film. The main drama concerns the factions and rivalry between Sgt Elias and Sgt Barnes observed by the sensitive college-educated Chris Taylor.

Since much of *Waltz with Bashir* revolves around present-day interviews, this sense of atmosphere that Chapman describes is equally crucial but not relayed in the same way as it is in films like *Platoon* or Stanley Kubrick's *Full Metal Jacket* (1987), the first half of which shows the brutal brain washing routine of a US marine boot camp that ends in a blood-spattered show down. In these movies, the mood of war pervades the entire film, whereas in Folman's film it is only evidenced during the flashbacks, many of which convey an atmosphere of random, unnecessary violence and time wasting. However, unlike *Full Metal Jacket* and *Apocalypse Now*, the war scenes are especially emotive precisely because they are flashbacks and therefore constitute the subjects' most troubling memories. In some instances, as in Folman's repeated vision, the flashback might not even be of a real event but is rather– at least according to Sivan –a symbolic representation of fear. If Sivan's diagnosis is accurate then this more than anything exemplifies the atmosphere and the horror of war.

More importantly, as I said in Chapter Two, *Waltz with Bashir* contains almost no historical or political context. The 1982 First Lebanon War was one of many major conflicts within the region and the result of a complex political impasse between the Israeli government and the Palestinian Liberation Organisation, backed by Syria. The Israelis had brokered a fragile allegiance with the Lebanese Christians, led by Bashir Gemayel on the assumption that once he was elected, Lebanon would become more pro-Israel. None of this is mentioned in the film and to the viewer with little knowledge of the region, names that are mentioned like 'Palestinians', 'Phalangists', 'Lebanon', 'Ariel Sharon', and 'Beirut' would probably mean very little.

You could argue that any explanation would be necessarily reductive, thereby compromising any responsible representation of the war. And the Israeli-Palestinian conflict is complicated enough without bringing in other players such as Syria and Lebanon. However, the lack of historical context or explanation might have another, more problematic, function other than making life easier for the viewer. Benziman argues that making a film such as *Waltz with Bashir* so long after the event creates the impression that the 1982 war was a one-time incident that is now finished, when in fact the Second Lebanon War broke out in 2006 and the repercussions of both wars can still be felt. More importantly, argues Benziman:

...the main thing missing from the movies is not just the historical-political context, but chiefly that of the ongoing political atmosphere in Israel and the inability to project the *Lebanon situation* onto other situations and draw conclusions from it.[25]

The retrospective viewpoint of Folman's film, which creates a narrative of traumatic event first, memory later, frames the 1982 war as a shameful episode in Israel's history that is now being dealt with. The reality is that atrocities continue to be perpetrated by the Israelis against the Palestinians, and Israel's role in the Sabra and Shatila massacre has never really been out of the public eye. Israel's part in the massacre (indirect though it was) is not simply a ghost from the past, but it continues to haunt the present. This is of course one of the crucial ways in which the Israel Vietnam comparison collapses because America is no longer involved in Vietnam – it really was a onetime event.[26] It is not surprising that while *Waltz with Bashir* ends upon a very sobering note – namely, processing the atrocities of the past has only just begun – the Vietnam films end with a sense of finality and usually more optimism. Although the final words of *Apocalypse Now* are 'The horror, the horror!' the closing scenes show Willard sailing away from the commune with his comrade; the mission is completed, Kurtz is dead and the rain is falling as though to cleanse away the actions of the past. Even the unreliable radio now works, to indicate that things are back to normal. *Platoon* meanwhile ends on a very overt note of optimism and of looking forward to the future. As Chris Taylor ascends in a medical helicopter into a very bright white light his voiceover announces:

'...those of us that did make it have an obligation to build again, to teach to others what we know, and to try with what's left of our lives to find a goodness and a meaning to this life.'[27]

This affirmation of life is repeated to some extent in Kubrick's *Full Metal Jacket*, which ends with the soldiers singing an upbeat troop song ('M.I.C.K.E.Y. M.O.U.S.E! We play fair and we work hard and we're in harmony'). Of course this song references the famous American TV show 'The Mickey Mouse Club', the lyrics of which are: 'Who's the leader of the club that's made for you and me: M.I.C.K.E.Y. M.O.U.S.E!' The upbeat nature of the troop's song is therefore tinged with mockery; the soldiers may be cheerful but they're not to be taken seriously. Or rather, the soldiers don't even take themselves seriously. The optimism with which the film ends is therefore a dubious one. At the same time we hear a voiceover that could also be interpreted as ironic: Private Joker's heartfelt declaration of life and a farewell to the past:

> 'We have nailed our names in the pages of history. Enough for today...I am so happy I am alive...I am in a world of shit, yes, but I am alive, and I am not afraid.'[28]

In all three Vietnam films the final scenes show the protagonists moving away from the scene of conflict, whereas in *Waltz with Bashir* the Folman character faces it head on. Nevertheless, as I said before, *Waltz with Bashir* still maintains a 'past is the past' viewpoint because it is about coming to terms with what has happened and learning from it. The learning might take place now but the events of Sabra and Shatila are still presented as over and done with.

Interestingly, Folman began research for his film in 2006, the year that the Second Lebanon War started. The fact that this later conflict is not mentioned in *Waltz with Bashir* reinforces the idea that the 1982 conflict is presented out of time, as an event that has already been and gone. Even if Folman had been inspired to make *Waltz with Bashir* because of the renewed conflict this is not represented in the film itself. Benziman's point is that because Folman's movie ends dramatically with live footage it creates the false impression that this is a traumatic image from the past that has been repressed and invisible. In fact, the image of screaming Palestinians alongside their dead is tragically a frequent one that takes place even now and also in the present-day of *Waltz with Bashir*, at the same time that Folman is interviewing his comrades. Naira Antoun, writing for *The Electronic Intifada* in February 2009 pointed out that:

> ...we are witnessing a perverse moment: an apparently 'anti-war' Israeli film wins several Israeli and international film awards in a context not only of Israel's ongoing brutal occupation, violations of international law, racism and denial of refugee rights, but also while fresh atrocities are committed by Israeli forces in Gaza...Indeed, the same Israelis who flocked to see the film gave their enthusiastic approval to Operation Cast Lead in Gaza.[29]

Interestingly enough, while the present-tenseness of the Palestinians' plight might not be obvious to the audience, the use of colour news footage in the final scene obliquely alludes to it – though perhaps unintentionally. News is by definition current, unlike live-action filming or animation which are created over an extended period of time; moreover, the fact that the repeated screams of the Palestinian women are not translated from the Arabic into either Hebrew or English singles out the footage from the rest of the otherwise meticulously edited film. Of course, *Waltz with Bashir* uses the present-tenseness of the footage to depict the protagonist's sudden and very all-consuming recollection of his time in Lebanon, whereby suddenly he is re-living the moment as though it were in the present. It is presumably not used to alert the viewer to the current circumstances of Palestinian refugees.

Anti-war cinema also has specific archetypes such as the innocent recruit and the tough commander. The most obvious example of this is the first half of *Full Metal Jacket* which, as we said earlier, depicts life on a US marine training camp. Sergeant Hartman is the mean and abusive commander who relentlessly humiliates his recruits in the name of training. One recruit in particular, nicknamed Captain Pyle, is mentally challenged and is therefore innocence and naivety personified. Though starting off as a seemingly smiley and happy-go lucky character Pyle is so badly bullied that he gradually transforms into a maniacal military robot, killing Hartman (using a full metal jacket) and then himself. Pyle therefore never makes it to Vietnam; he is broken by training before he can even get there.

In *Waltz with Bashir* the sergeants in command are apathetic rather than bullying – for instance, the previously mentioned porn-watching commander in the Lebanese villa – or invisible, as in Boaz's superior who tells him to shoot the village dogs. But there are several instances of the so-called wide-eyed recruit. When the Folman character first interviews Carmi Canaan he says: 'For 18 you seemed pretty bright to me. I never took you for a fighter'.[30] This is quite a strange comment because it implies that Canaan had a choice whether or not to participate in the fighting. Presumably Folman is referring to Carmi's general enthusiasm about fighting. But the comment is also odd because it excludes Folman from the equation. Folman might have amnesia but he knows for a fact he was in Lebanon; is this because he isn't bright? Is he hoping that he rebelled but forgot about it? The suggestion that Carmi was bright and therefore had a choice initially challenges Carmi's (and by extension, Israel's) actions; but then this is toned down when Folman neglects to say anything critical after the interview.

Carmi responds to Folman's query in the mode of 'innocent recruit'. He was a nerd with masculinity issues and he wanted to prove to everyone that he could be a brave hero. Unfortunately, as soon as he realised he might be in danger he threw up everywhere and passed out. This immediately tells the viewer that Carmi was unfit for military combat; he was a sheep in wolf's clothing, put in a combat zone by accident. Even though he had wanted to prove his masculinity the audience realises that being a soldier is a completely unnatural state for Carmi. This expression of sensitivity obfuscates the violence of the following scene in which Carmi, from sheer panic and fear, shoots dead a whole family of Palestinians in their car.

Likewise, the quiet and nervous looking Ronny Dayag tells Folman that when they began their incursion into Lebanon it felt as if they were on holiday. They ate crisps, told jokes and took photos, seemingly oblivious to the bloodshed that awaited them. He talks about the beautiful view and how they were able to enjoy the idyllic surroundings. Even though Dayag's flashback shows Israeli tanks in Lebanon crushing civilian cars and smashing shopping windows, his testimony is one of innocence and bewilderment. He describes the ambush that takes place later on the beach in terms of victimhood; there is no acknowledgment that the ambush might have been provoked by the Israelis. He continues his testimony using terms of sensitivity and pathos:

> I felt abandoned by our forces. I imagined how my mother would react. We're very close. I was always like her right hand. I'm the only one who helps out at home.[31]

In the above quotation Dayag presents himself as a helpless pawn of the Israeli army, left defenceless, still an innocent child missing his family. The accompanying images of a sweet little boy cuddling his mother are poignant to say the least, and the audience is required to empathise with this loving bond, now threatened by the ambush. Again, whilst Dayag's testimony encourages anti-war sentiments, these sentiments are one-sided and centre on the suffering of the everyday Israeli who has to risk his life in the name of national security. You would never guess from Dayag's account that Israel actually chose to enter Lebanon.

Fig. 12: Carmi shown vomiting on deck

Fig. 13: Dayag thinking about his mother

According to these testimonies, and others, such as the traumatised Boaz Buskila-Rein, *Waltz with Bashir* suggests that during the 1982 war the new Israeli recruit was a sensitive soul rather than a gung-ho patriot and the IDF command was a brutal, unthinking machine that administered orders cruelly, as with the execution of the twenty-six dogs, and often arbitrarily, as with the red Mercedes. Whilst this reinforces the notion of anti-war archetypes, the Israeli soldiers nevertheless obeyed their commanders; there is no sense of rebellion as in Private Pyle and the scornful Private Joker in *Full Metal Jacket* or Captain Kurtz in *Apocalypse Now*. The only real anti-war message in *Waltz with Bashir* is the horrific live footage at the end, yet even this is understood to be the result of Phalangist, not Israeli brutality. Folman may condemn Israeli inactivity during the Sabra and Shatila massacres, but he never condemns Israel's presence in Lebanon because he never offers any historical or political context in which to do so. In this sense, describing Folman's film as anti-war is misleading because the viewer isn't actually told what the war is. The anti-war message is in fact anti-violence and anti-terror, but not really anti-war.

Now that we have looked at *Waltz with Bashir* through the lens of American Vietnam movies I would like to briefly consider another point of reference, namely animated films that deal with war scenarios, in particular *Barefoot Gen* (Mori Masaki, 1983), *When the Wind Blows* (Jimmy Murakami, 1986) and *Grave of the Fireflies* (Isao Takahata, 1988).

Both *Barefoot Gen* and *Grave of the Fireflies* are based on historical events that took place in Japan 1945; the latter right after the US Kobe bombing and the former during the US atomic attack of Hiroshima and Nagasaki. *When the Wind Blows* takes place in an imaginary 1980s Britain preparing for and then suffering a Soviet nuclear missile attack. All three films centre on the experiences of civilians rather than soldiers or the military and all three are based upon either graphic novels or comics (*Barefoot Gen* by Keiji Nakazawa, *When the Wind Blows* by Raymond Briggs) or autobiographical stories (*Grave of the Fireflies* by Akiyuki Nosaka).

All three have also been described as anti-war – *Barefoot Gen* is a key anti-war text in Japanese elementary schools – though they differ in their delivery.[32] Susan Napier argues that *Grave of the Fireflies* is ultimately a tale of passivity and victimhood and a completely de masculinised Japan, whilst *Barefoot Gen* conveys hope and resilience in the face of adversity. Even more than Nakazawa's film, *When the Wind Blows* is the ultimate example of fortitude and strength in times of hardship, on occasion to the point of absurdity. The protagonists Jim and Hilda Bloggs have placed full trust in the British government and its ability to protect them from a nuclear attack. Even when they are both dying of radiation poisoning this trust never wavers; it is only at the end of the film, as they both succumb to death, that they turn their hopes away from Britain to God.

As with *Waltz with Bashir*, none of the films acknowledge the historical contexts that led to the traumatic events described – Japanese aggression against China; the Japanese bombing of Pearl Harbour.[33] In the case of *When the Wind Blows*, which is not based upon fact but possible scenarios, there is almost no explanation of what might have led to a Soviet attack, i.e. an alternative Cold War scenario. All we know is that Jim Bloggs fought against the 'Jerries' during the forties and now it is the 'Ruskies' that are a threat. Politicians are repeatedly referred to as 'the powers that be' and Jim has no recollection of who the Prime Minister is.

The same questions asked of *Waltz with Bashir* have also been asked of these films: what is the effect of animation? Why use animation? Is animation the best medium with which to convey events? In the case of *Barefoot Gen* and *When the Wind Blows* animation has very specific functions: to convey what seems beyond words, namely, the unimaginable horror of the atomic bomb. Napier discusses this with special reference to the scene in *Barefoot Gen* where we see the effects of the atomic missile:

> Most memorable is the image of the little girl...as she turns instantaneously from a 'realistic' cartoon character into a damned soul from Buddhist mythology, a 'walking ghost', hair on fire, eyes popping out, and fingers melting into hideously extended tendrils.[34]

Crucially, the distancing effect of the animation allows the viewer to watch traumatic scenes such as these and yet still return to the narrative afterwards.[35] Perhaps therefore, animation's distancing effect is its most important function: it allows the viewer to become a witness to history's most excruciating events without the accompanying trauma. The fact that animation can convey unimaginable horrors such as human transmogrification is only secondary; after all, *Grave of the Fireflies* is not about nuclear war, but about the slow and pitiful demise of two young children. Most of the scenes in Takahata's film could conceivably be rendered in live action, so the decision to use animation must address some other need, namely a 'psychological buffer zone' for the viewer.[36]

However, if we were to search for an equivalent scene in *Waltz with Bashir*, where war victims sustain horrific injury, then it would be the massacre at Sabra and Shatila, but this is never represented in Folman's film. Aside from a few gun shots we never witness the massacre because *Waltz with Bashir* isn't told from the victims' perspective and Folman clearly wasn't present within the camps at the time. In fact, if you were to

Fig. 14: transmogrification scene in Barefoot Gen

compare *Waltz with Bashir* with any of the films mentioned – both the Vietnam movies and the animated ones – there are relatively few scenes of graphic violence and bloodshed. In the case of Folman's film, the 'unconveyable' consists mainly of psychological trauma; animation therefore has a penetrative function that allows the viewer to enter the troubled minds of the protagonists. It permits entry into their fantasies and fears and nightmares. Since we are not sure how many of these fantasies and fears are grounded in fact, the use of animation compliments the imaginative aspect of the film. When we see Carmi's flashback for instance, where he passes out on a ship and hallucinates in shades of icy green and blue that a giant inflatable woman rescues him from the sea, what we see is a creative interpretation of his testimony. And as it's a flashback of a hallucination rather than a 'real' event there are no limits to how it should be conveyed. What we get is a bird's eye view, shrouded in mist, of a gigantesque female swimming back stroke towards the boat. The aerial perspective shows her approaching the boat, which looks miniscule by comparison and in the background we hear the haunting Max Richter score. Moreover, the animation allows for the convincing portrayal of a surreal image – a tiny Carmi floating away astride the large inflatable woman – that might otherwise look ridiculous in live action. This is also true of the Folman character's recurring vision where he and his comrades emerge naked from the sea and walk in painfully slow motion towards the shore. In live action this scene would risk resembling a zombie movie rather than a long repressed vision.

Compared to *Waltz with Bashir*'s very frequent and surreal flashbacks, *Grave of the Fireflies*, *Barefoot Gen*, or *When the Wind Blows* depict chiefly realistic scenes; the difference is that if you were to try and film the immediate effects of radiation and the atomic bomb using live action it would probably be impossible without special effects. Ironically, the animation makes these horrific scenes that actually took place in 1945 more convincing than they would be otherwise in live action. In Jimmy Murakami's film, the animation also allows for a privileged aerial perspective of the bomb's impact: we see sheep rolling over hills like cotton wool buds; trees and houses exploding; a train veering off a collapsing bridge. At one point we even become the eye of the bomb and we hurtle at breakneck speed towards the house of Jim and Hilda Bloggs.

To sum up, *Waltz with Bashir* can be read within the context of anti-war movies, as described by James Chapman. It has a particular affinity with American films about Vietnam such *Apocalypse Now*, *Full Metal Jacket* and *Platoon*. Several common anti-war themes and archetypes present within the Vietnam film cycle – *Apocalypse Now*, in particular –can also be applied to Folman's film: moral confusion; internal conflict; dissociation from any historical context; and the dynamic between the innocent recruit and the tough commander. *Waltz with Bashir* can also be compared to animated films that deal with war scenarios, in particular *Barefoot Gen*, *When the Wind Blows* and *Grave of the Fireflies*.

References

1.   James Chapman, *War and Film* (London: Reaktion, 2008), p. 9.

2.   Chapman, ibid., p. 117.

3.   Michael Sragow, 'A step-by-step illustration of war', *Baltimore Sun*, (2009).

4.   Peter Travers, 'Waltz with Bashir', *Rolling Stone*, (2009).

5.   Rene Rodriguez, 'Trying to remember a nightmare', *Miami Herald* (2009).

6.   Peter Bradshaw, '*Waltz with Bashir*', *The Guardian*, (2008)

7.   Jonathan Freedland, 'Lest we forget', *The Guardian*, (2008).

8.   David Ansen, '*Waltz with Bashir*', *Newsweek*, (2008).

9.   Jonathan Curiel, '*Waltz with Bashir*', *San Francisco Chronicle* (2009).

10. Chapman, pp. 160-61.

11. Hillel Halkin, 'The *Waltz with Bashir* Two-Step', *Commentary*, (March 2009), p. 51.

12. See Yuval Benziman, 'Mom, I'm Home': Israeli Lebanon-War Films as Inadvertent Preservers of the National Narrative', *Israel Studies*, (Fall 2013), p. 116.

13. Ella Shohat, *Israeli Cinema: East/West and the Politics of Representation* (London: IB Tauris), p. 232.

14. Benziman, op. cit., p. 11.

15. Chapman, op. cit., p. 117.

16. *Apocalypse Now*

17. *Waltz with Bashir*, 00:58:54

18. Chapman, p. 166.

19. Benziman, op. cit. pp. 8-11.

20. Benziman, p. 11.

21. *Waltz with Bashir*, 00:23:30

22. Chapman, p. 164.

23. This is Benziman's argument. See p. 14.

24. Chapman, p. 166.

25. Benziman, p. 16.

26. See Arthur Bradley, 'Israel's Vietnam: Framing the Lebanese War' in Thomas Austenfeld (ed.), *Terrorism and Narrative Practise* (Münster: LIT Verlag, 2011), pp. 219-235.

27. *Platoon*, (Oliver Stone, 1986), 01:50:19.

28. *Full Metal Jacket*, (Stanley Kubrick, 1987), 01:46:42.

29. Naira Antoun, '*Waltz with Bashir*', *The Electronic Intifada* (2009)

30. *Waltz with Bashir*, 00:15:51.

31. Ibid., 00:30:36.

32. See Susan Napier, 'No More Words: *Barefoot Gen*, *Grave of the Fireflies*, and 'Victim's History'' in Napier, *Anime: from Akira to Howl's Moving Castle* (New York and Basingstoke: Palgrave Macmillan, 2005), pp. 217-231.

33. Ibid., pp. 218-221.

34. Ibid., p. 225.

35. Ibid., p. 222.

36. Ibid., p. 223.

Chapter Five: Ari Folman's Other War

There's a chance that if you watched *Waltz with Bashir* just once you might have completely missed any references to the Holocaust. They are exceptionally brief and take place only towards the end of the film. Furthermore, as we shall see, the first two are mentioned in the context of a friendly chat with Folman's 'therapist' friend. The third reference to the film, made by journalist Ben-Yishai, is also brief though pertinent.

But if you study *Waltz with Bashir* carefully, the references to the Holocaust, though sparsely and cautiously embedded, are fundamental to an understanding of the film. As I have demonstrated in Chapter Four *Waltz with Bashir* is chiefly about the 1982 First Lebanon war, and in particular, the Sabra and Shatila massacres. It is about one soldier's attempt to recall his activities during this time. But this attempt and its results are tempered by the film's references to the Shoah. The question is: Why are the references there? And why are they there in such a wishy-washy way? If you are going to imply that Israel's military activity is affected by Jewish history or that Jewish history can be revisited by current Israeli activity then why whisper about it? This in itself is very strange. Furthermore, Folman's shy allusions to the Holocaust contrast significantly with those made by other second generation film makers that tackle the subject head-on. In this chapter I consider all these issues and ask: what then is the function of the Holocaust in the film?

The Legacy of the Holocaust in Israeli Cinema

The representation of war in Israeli cinema has followed a fairly clear path. This path is both chronological – following the course of the major wars fought in Israel – and thematic, reflecting shifts in public opinion regarding these wars.[1] This is intertwined with another trajectory, namely the representation of the Holocaust within Israeli cinema. Whilst several films exploring the impact of the Shoah are unrelated to the subject of war, (that is, some just focus on the survivors' experiences in Israel), others are concerned with the interrelationship between the trauma of the Jewish experience in Europe and the conduct of war in Israel. Understandably, this interrelationship has evolved and developed over the years along with shifts in cultural and social responses towards the Holocaust in Israel.

In the late 1940s and 1950s the predominant representation of the Holocaust was in terms of 'negation of exile'.[2] This term, which has been widely discussed by Israeli and Jewish historians, refers to the rejection of the 'Jewish culture of exile'. The Jewish culture of exile sees the dispersion of Jews among nations other than Israel as a central feature of Jewish identity.[3] According to this view the Jew is forever wandering, forever the stranger, and cut off from his spiritual home in the Holy Land.

Zionists felt that that this culture of exile was the root of the so-called Jewish problem and called for it to be eradicated. So, for example, in the Israeli film *Hill 24 Doesn't Answer* (Thorold Dickinson, 1955), which is set during Israel's War of Independence, the figure of the *Sabra* (native Israeli) officer is momentarily replaced by that of a meek ghetto Jew precisely at the moment when the same officer is about to kill his enemy.[4] Although much could be said about this particular scene, the essential message is that the trauma of the Holocaust experience has to be contained in order to survive and to build a new Jewish homeland.

During the sixties and seventies there were very few references to the Holocaust in Israeli cinema and even less to its significance in regard to modern Israeli warfare.[5] The two exceptions are *Operation Jonathan* (Menahem Golan, 1977) and *The Wooden Gun* (Ilan Moshenson, 1979). The latter is of particular interest for this chapter because it reverses the message of *Hill 24 Doesn't Answer* and condemns the use of brutality in combat, revealing that this brutality is futile and immoral.

The eighties and nineties marked the emergence of second generation Israeli cinema, specifically produced by children of survivors. Second generation films, whilst not directly addressing the subject of war, often critiqued Zionism (the project to build a home for the Jews in Palestine), suggesting that it had simply replaced the trauma of the Holocaust with a new and different kind of Israeli trauma.[6]

The representation of the Holocaust in Israeli cinema during the first decade of the new millennium, the period most relevant to our discussion, suggests ambivalence towards the legacy of the Holocaust upon modern Israeli identity. According to Ilan Avisar this ambivalence centres on the theme of revenge: more precisely, Jewish Israeli revenge on Nazi war criminals and the question of whether this revenge is at all useful or justified.[7] As we saw in Chapter One, Folman's film *Made in Israel* (2001), which considers how the Jewish people might take revenge on a Nazi war criminal, is a perfect example of this ambivalence. Whilst this chapter doesn't focus specifically on the question of revenge in *Waltz with Bashir*, it does address the nature of ambivalence with regard to the Holocaust and modern Israeli identity.

In this chapter I look at how *Waltz with Bashir*'s direct engagement with the Sabra and Shatila massacres is destabilised by an indirect Holocaust narrative that is planted in the film though never substantiated. This takes place during three key points within the film. The two narratives (Lebanon and the Shoah) are sustained by the film's mode of representation, namely animation with documentary features. It is this mode that distinguishes *Waltz with Bashir* from other Israeli films that address the events of 1982 – i.e. *Cup Final* (Eran Riklis, 1991) and *Lebanon* (Samuel Maoz, 2009) – films that use narrative fiction rather than documentary or animation, and do not go beyond Israel's very recent political and military past.[8]

In fact, the film's sporadic and fleeting references to the Holocaust alongside Folman's own biography (son of Holocaust survivors) possibly place it within another filmic tradition, namely that of documentaries made by second generation filmmakers. These include Orna Ben Dor's *Because of That War* (1988), Tzipi Reibenbach's *Choice and Destiny* (1993) and Asher Tlalim's *Don't Touch My Holocaust* (1994).[9]

The intertwining of these two filmic traditions in *Waltz with Bashir* – fictional portrayal of 1982 and second generation documentary centring on the Holocaust experience – isn't that surprising: post Zionist revisionism, which criticises Zionism's standardising of Holocaust memory for the purpose of national interest, was partly triggered by the Lebanon invasion and had a large influence upon second generation culture. This is because Israel's unnecessary and ill-fated invasion in 1982 revealed flaws in the country's vision of itself. The previously accepted narrative of a noble State of Israel that was forged out of Holocaust trauma, and only fought when attacked, was undermined by Israel's behaviour in Lebanon, in particular the Sabra and Shatila massacre. So Folman's desire to relate to his parents' experiences at Auschwitz, coupled with his guilt about his role in Lebanon, typify some of the anxieties associated with second generation Israelis.

Of course, the three documentaries mentioned above – *Because of That War*, *Choice and Destiny*, *Don't Touch My Holocaust* – deal directly with the Shoah and are not animated and, as such, *Waltz with Bashir* could only be regarded as an experimental example of this tradition.

I also examine what the purpose of this dual discourse – Lebanon and the Holocaust – might be. Does referring to the Holocaust, however briefly, mean that Folman's personal engagement with his role in Lebanon is always mediated by and therefore compromised by his status as a so-called second generation Israeli? Can Folman ever just think about his time in Lebanon without associating it (consciously or unconsciously) to the Nazis and the Holocaust? Does *Waltz with Bashir* show the past as a spectre that forever haunts the present? Is animation used to represent this spectral quality of history? Perhaps this last-but-one interpretation is a bit static and fatalistic: first, it suggests that nothing can be done to relieve the burden of history; second, it implies that the present is always doomed to sway under this burden.

Or perhaps, does alluding to the Holocaust show how our understanding of the distant past can actually be revised and reworked through the present, and that both, past and present, are in fact mutually beneficial? Does the animation then act as a type of fluidity between past and present? Can the distant past overlap with the present and cause small ripples in both directions? I don't have a definitive answer but I think that the animation in *Waltz with Bashir* allows for the past and present to impact upon each other. I shall talk about this later in the chapter. Let us now look more carefully at how the film's form allows for an exploration of both Lebanon and the Holocaust that is unfixed and open ended.

As we know, *Waltz with Bashir* is a combination of animation, documentary and narrative fiction. On the one hand, it is based around interviews, but on the other, these interviews are based upon a screenplay and recorded in a studio. In the case of Carmi Canaan and Boaz Rein-Buskila, actors' voices were used instead of the interviewees, consequently undermining any claim to authentic interactive documentary.

The documentary form is also undermined by the fact that the interviews are at odds with the film's central hypothesis, namely that the Israeli government was indirectly complicit in the massacres and that the Israeli soldiers – Folman included – were aware of atrocities taking place. This damning conclusion is at odds with how Folman conducts the film: the majority of witnesses in *Waltz with Bashir* are his friends and are presented favourably, as though they were simply victims of circumstance. Dror Harazi is the one exception; he is grilled by Folman about his role in the massacre. The interview style is important because theoretically everyone Folman interviews should be treated the same. Meanwhile, Folman's own amnesia protects him from any kind of cross-examination. There is therefore a clash of the film's friendly interview styles with its central message concerning Israel and Lebanon.

Fig. 15: Carmi and Folman relaxing in the living-room with a joint

Fig.16: Frenkel showing Folman how to use patchouli oil

Fig. 17: Folman and Dayag sitting next to each other in Dayag's office

This clash is further complicated by the three brief references in the film to the Shoah: the first two, as we know, are made by Ori Sivan to Folman; the final one is made by the journalist Ron Ben-Yishai, who compares a scene to the liberation of the Warsaw Ghetto. Let us focus on the first two references, during which Sivan argues that Folman has unconsciously associated himself with the Nazis. It is crucial that not only is Sivan not actually a real therapist (he is never described as a professional therapist in the film) but Folman never expresses an opinion about Sivan's diagnosis. This diagnosis which therefore crucially remains unsubstantiated by Folman comes almost at the end of the film and therefore colours everything that has come before: interviews, conversations, testimonies, and flashbacks. Now it seems that a dual query has taken place: first to see what happened in Lebanon; second to work out if the Israeli soldiers that stood by during the massacre are any different from the Nazis.

But as I have stressed before, the fact that Folman only smiles vaguely when Sivan offers his Holocaust diagnosis is important. Both the Folman character, and therefore *Waltz with Bashir* are seemingly noncommittal about the function of Folman's second generation identity in his investigation about Lebanon. While some scholars, such as Raya Morag, have taken the diagnosis as fact and argued that it constitutes a type of denial about Lebanon, you could also argue that Folman's silence is actually a type of shyness or embarrassment about the link to the Shoah.[10] Of course, embarrassed silence or not, the Holocaust reference is part of the film and therefore explicitly asks the viewer to add it to the equation.

Importantly, Folman's investigation into the atrocities in Lebanon is coded as both civilised and rational, masking the monstrous nature of the crimes that Folman is investigating and further accentuating the bizarre clash of hypothesis and interview style. This civilising process is evident from the highly orchestrated settings in which each conversation or interview takes place. This, of course, occurs in live-action documentary, but in animation, where each and every detail has to be drawn, it is even more pronounced. In the opening scene, for example, Boaz describes his horrific experiences in a cosy dimly-lit bar surrounded by music and film posters where other customers are sitting quietly chatting amongst themselves; Folman's 'psychiatrist' friend reassuringly always has a chessboard or a *New Yorker* magazine next to him, and Carmi recounts frightening episodes by the fireside in an old European-style room with a leather sofa, wooden table and glass cabinets filled with books. Even Folman's voiceover account of a particularly bloody episode during which Frenkel is shooting in all directions is softened by the comparison to a waltz. Indeed, Chopin's 'Waltz in C Sharp Minor' begins even as Frenkel's interview comes to a close. Consequently, the present day interview scene seems to overlap with the past, to a balletic sequence where he is dancing amongst bullets whilst Lebanese civilians are watching from balconies, as if at the theatre.[11] These various juxtapositions of present day civility and past atrocity remind the viewer that the Lebanon war, like the Shoah, has to an extent been naturalised as past history, even if, like the Shoah, it still affects those individuals that were involved.

The hazy nature of the film's message and hypothesis is also strengthened by the fact that Folman visually 'owns' each and every testimony. As we know, in live-action documentary, the interviewee is filmed by a camera. Aside from lighting and sound there is nothing else that mediates what is between the subject and the audience. By contrast, animation is constructed according to the wishes of the animator and is totally subjective. The animator who draws a man being interviewed cannot be one hundred per cent objective. He draws what he sees, and the drawing would be different from what any other animator would come up with, even if they were sitting in the same spot.

An example of how Folman visually 'owns' each and every testimony is when Folman first visits Ori Sivan. Whilst the two men are chatting about amnesia, Sivan demonstrates the process of false memory by describing a well-known experiment. In this experiment a group of people are shown ten childhood images relating to a visit to Luna Park.[12] Luna Park is a generic name for 'amusement park' but it is also a brand name that originated in 1903. There is a large and famous Luna Park in Tel Aviv, which opened in 1970, and it is likely that an Israeli watching *Waltz with Bashir* would have this place in mind when hearing the term.

Although Sivan does not give verbal examples of the ten childhood images used in the experiment, we the audience are presented with a selection that seems completely incompatible with the term 'Luna Park' and also to the film's imagery in general: we see a rural European landscape gradually being filled with an array of figures. A small selection of these are dressed in clothes typical of 1950s America – a young girl in a sailor's suit eating candy floss with her boyfriend, a large man in T-shirt and trousers eating an ice-cream and a man in a suit next to a 'shoot house'. Yet, most of the figures appear to date from 1940s Europe – men in dark double breasted suits, women in long coats and cloche hats – whilst the person hypothetically undergoing the experiment is presented as a little boy in old-fashioned knickerbockers carrying a pink balloon. Furthermore, whilst the American figures are completely expressionless, those from Europe are staged in a comparatively dramatic manner: one of the men is staring into the distance, seemingly at a very mournful mother and daughter; next to him, a woman in a grey outfit is standing with her back to the viewer as though looking for someone.

In other words, the imaginary childhood that appears to us is far removed from the childhood that Folman, who was born in 1962, would have experienced. The 'Luna Park' that appears to us is inhabited by individuals from his parents' generation, from wartime Europe and post-war America. This means that Sivan's description of a famous experiment, where participants are shown pictures of a generic amusement park, is completely subordinated to Folman's own vision. We, the viewer, hear Sivan describe an experiment about 'Luna Park', a place which would be well known to a contemporary Israeli viewer, but what we see comes from Folman's mind, not Sivan's description.

Fig. 18: Fairground

It is definitely interesting that during an experiment concerning false memory the imagined childhood should contain so many scenes of wartime Europe. A fundamental characteristic of the second generation is that even though they may have inherited a sense of exile from their parents (exile from Europe), they will never know or understand the Europe from which this exile took place.[13] They know that they should mourn a lost Europe, but their mourning will always be incomplete because it is for something they never really knew. They can only retrieve this 'knowledge' or 'memory' via their imagination. *Waltz with Bashir* is premised upon the significance of recovering memory, although it is only later that this is connected to the Holocaust.

There are therefore two concurrent processes taking place at Sivan's house: the first is the interview with Sivan, in which Folman says he can't remember his exact whereabouts and activities at the time of the massacres; the second is the hypothetical experiment where, unknown to Sivan but not the viewer, Folman imagines a scene that he could never have experienced. At one point during their conversation, animation allows the two processes to overlap and behind Folman we see the imagined (and old-fashioned) fairground scene through the window.

The two processes are crucially different. Folman's amnesia suggests denial, whilst the scene with the old-fashioned figures alludes to an over-determined Zionism that can be described in the following way: since Jewish life in Europe has been irreparably damaged, there is no choice but to establish a Jewish state. In other words the nostalgic nature of

Folman's 'false memory' could be read as a justification for both Folman's past activities and the way in which he subsequently deals with these activities. Yes, he may have repressed his activities in Lebanon but he (and Israel as a whole) is still haunted by the tragic losses of Jewish history. This points to an overarching narrative within the film: the desire to reconcile a long-lost past with recent history, and the way this desire both validates and condemns Israeli military activity.

We can also see how Folman's vision permeates the entire film in the editing of the interviews, especially the final two. This editing impacts the investigation into Lebanon but also the less direct investigation into the Holocaust. As I said earlier, the first eight interviews are conducted as informal conversations whereby the implied film maker, Ari Folman, is a character within the animation. The style of conversation is polite and non-confrontational (and usually involves a jovial drink of some sort) and each of the witnesses' testimonies is privileged with its own animation sequence.

However, the final testimonies are of particular interest, not least because unlike all the other interviews, they are filmed against a completely bare background as though to minimise distractions. The first is with veteran war journalist Ron Ben-Yishai, the second interview is with an Israeli soldier, Dror Harazi.

We know from chapter three that the discrepancy between the two interview styles is curious. When Harazi tells Folman what happened at the Sabra and Shatila camps Folman repeatedly questions him, but this is absolutely not the case with the veteran journalist. Ben-Yishai tells Folman that he heard rumours of a possible massacre in the camps but then he returned home and made dinner for his friends. Then, whilst at dinner, says Ben-Yishai, the regiment commander also told him that a massacre had taken place.

Later that night, after dinner, Ben-Yishai tells Folman that he rang Defence Minister Ariel Sharon to tell him about the massacres but that Sharon seemed unperturbed. Ben-Yishai was disappointed but nevertheless waited until the next morning before investigating further.

Not only does Folman neglect to query Ben-Yishai's passivity, but he treats the journalist's shocked testimony of entering the destroyed camps

Fig. 19: Yishai hearing about the massacre at a dinner party

as a catalyst for the entire film. This catalyst is expressed in the form of live footage and seemingly embodies the moment when Folman's repressed trauma has come to the surface and he is overwhelmed by the full impact of his experiences. This catalyst appears to mark a moment of revelation when Folman and the audience experience events in an 'authentic' way. But this seeming moment of revelation is made problematic by Ben-Yishai's previous trust in the Israeli army and by his failure to honour his role as investigative correspondent.

In other words, the film's entire trajectory seems to move from a purely subjective or private mode to an allegedly objective and public one in the form of news footage; it is supposedly a move from the opaque to the transparent, but this move is grossly over-determined precisely because the footage is not as spontaneous or as radical as it purports to be. *Waltz with Bashir* cannot really be a linear narrative which begins with ignorance and climactically finishes with complete awareness because Ben-Yishai already knew about the massacres before he entered the camp. More crucially, he entered the camp precisely with the aim of filming the consequences of the massacre. He certainly didn't attempt to film the massacre itself.

This circularity also exists in Folman's own personal narrative, which is, of course, carefully and meticulously structured to describe an initial amnesia leading to total recall. The true source of this recall is unknown, although in narrative terms it is shown to coincide with the use of Ben-Yishai's testimony at the end. During this (still animated) testimony we see

Palestinian women leaving the camps but we hear what is, presumably, live audio footage of their screams. We follow the women's gaze as they walk up the street. Eventually they reach Folman and his comrade. For a few moments the camera lingers on the shocked expression of the two soldiers; then suddenly we see what the soldiers can see (the screaming women), and this is when the live visual footage begins. Therefore, according to the trajectory, amnesia equals animation, and full recollection equals 'reality' in the form of news footage.

As I have already intimated, the use of this live footage at the end of the film is misleading because it creates the false impression that reality has finally broken through, and that everything in the film until now has been doubtful, an artifice, or a mystery. It creates a structure of revelation, which is misleading because the thing that was revealed – namely the massacre and Folman's role in the massacre – was already known.

Alongside this circuitous discourse concerning Israel's involvement in the massacres, is a subtle though pertinent dialogue with Holocaust memory. When Ben-Yishai describes those Palestinians that survived the massacres he says the following:

> You know that picture from the Warsaw ghetto? The one with the kid holding his hands in the air? That's just how the long line of women, old people and children looked.[14]

Since the Warsaw photo in question belongs to imagery associated with the Nuremberg trial and with visual evidence of the Shoah, it has become an established icon of post-Holocaust memory and a testimony to the eventual victory of 'good' over 'evil'. The fact that Ben-Yishai refers to this photo precisely at the moment when he and his cameramen are about to film the aftermath of the massacres endows his footage with an exaggerated and inauthentic gravitas that potentially releases him from any responsibility. By extension, it endows the Israeli media with similarly exaggerated noble qualities.

So why is the reference to the Warsaw ghetto significant for our discussion? How does the juxtaposition of animation and live footage affect the dual investigation into Lebanon and the Holocaust? Is it possible that Folman's personal quest to recall his activities during the Lebanon War, which, as we have seen, is structured to progress from the

Fig. 20: Palestinian boy holding up arms like Warsaw photo

opaque to the transparent, is transformed into a moral victory by virtue
of the reference to Warsaw? In other words, does the reference tell the
audience that Folman has finally confronted his demons and that he is
taking responsibility for his actions? Does the reference represent a moral
victory for the Israeli media that transmitted the terrible scenes to the
world?

Or, conversely, is it the film's supposed inquiry into the Shoah that is
impacted by the final scenes in which we see both animated and live
images of the surviving Palestinians as well as the corpses? If so then
perhaps these final scenes function as a compensatory gesture that
temporarily alleviates the trauma of never being able to bear witness to
the Holocaust.

I would argue that both interpretations are central to the film, but only as
starting points for discussion rather than as fixed readings. As I suggested
earlier, the dual interrogation – the explicit attempt to recall recent events
in Lebanon and the implicit desire to understand the Holocaust – permits
greater understanding of modern Israeli identity and allows this identity
to be contextualised within a wider Jewish history. For instance, Folman's
journey from amnesia to recall can be read alongside another journey
in which his identity as Israeli citizen and soldier expands to that of a
second-generation Jew.

But I don't think the film is quite so simplistic, or that it would offer such
a diplomatic way out. It is not simply the case that the young eighteen-

year old Folman identified with the Nazis and consequently repressed his involvement in the Sabra and Shatila massacres. After all, the film is forthright in the brutal and horrific nature of this massacre. By contrast the horrors of the Shoah are barely touched upon.

On the other hand, as I discussed earlier, the nature of the interviews, with one exception, are sympathetic and favourable towards the witnesses and even more so to narrator-protagonist Folman, who is of course portrayed as an intelligent and sensitive investigator. Furthermore, although the film is clear about Israel's presence at the time of Sabra and Shatila, it also resolutely and categorically states that Israel was not responsible for the massacre. The IDF soldiers lit flares to guide the Phalangists but they didn't carry out the slaughter.

Rather, *Waltz with Bashir* embodies the complexities inherent within modern Israeli identity without pronouncing a final judgement. This fluidity is maintained both through the film's subject – a historical inquiry in which personal and collective histories are blurred – and form, whereby investigative journalism and therapy are queried via animation, which in turn is seemingly undermined by live footage.

Taking into account the film's ostensibly dual investigation into Lebanon and the Holocaust, the political implications of *Waltz with Bashir* are startling and disappointing: although it is admirable to strive for a comprehensive representation of historical and personal complexity, it is also safer than outright blame or regret. Fleeting references to the Nazis do not constitute full engagement with the trauma and significance of the Holocaust, and they minimise the impact of Folman's personal inquiry into Lebanon. Similarly, a few minutes of live footage showing murdered Palestinians cannot constitute engagement with the horrors of the massacre.

Even more worryingly, by aligning the Sabra and Shatila massacres with a distant European past, the film inadvertently closes off any considerations about the present and future tense of the Palestinians. The final scenes of live footage tell the audience that a breakthrough has been achieved; Folman has now fully remembered and come to terms with the past. The future can only get better because Folman is confronting his past. Folman's future has become clear, the cobwebs of amnesia now swept away.

Fig. 21: Palestinian women screaming and crying with no subtitles

Indeed, Folman's future does become brighter for having remembered. We know this because he was able to make the film. Importantly, his revelation would not have surprised any Israeli viewers because by the time *Waltz with Bashir* came out, the country's complicity in the massacres was well known. This fact emphasises the personal nature of the film – *Waltz with Bashir* really is just about one man. And perhaps (I say this controversially) it also emphasises the futility of the film's climactic ending. In 1982 we may have watched weeping Palestinian women on television and then forgot about it. Why should it be any different this time?

References

1. Uri S. Cohen, 'From Hill to Hill: A Brief History of the Representation of War in Israeli Cinema,' in *Israeli Cinema: Identities in Motion*, ed. Miri Talmon and Yaron Peleg (Austin: University of Texas Press, 2011), 43-55. See also: Nitzan Ben-Shaul, *Mythical Expressions of Siege in Israeli Films* (New York: Edwin Mellen, 1987) and Judd Ne'eman, 'The Death Mask of the Moderns: A Genealogy of New Sensibility Cinema in Israel,' *Israel Studies* 4 (1) (Spring 1999): 100-128.

2. Ilan Avisar, 'The Holocaust in Israeli Cinema as Conflict between Survival and Morality,' in *Israeli Cinema: Identities in Motion*, 153.

3. The Diaspora refers to countries other than Israel where Jews live. See Sandra Meiri, 'The Foreigner Within and the Question of Identity in *Fictitious Marriage and Streets of Yesterday*,' in *Israeli Cinema: Identities in Motion* op.cit., note 3, p. 253.

4. Ibid., p. 154.

5. Ibid., p. 155.

6.   Ibid., 159-160.

7.   Ibid., 160-164. Moreover, Avisar describes *Waltz with Bashir* as a revenge narrative, although he doesn't explain why and it is for this reason I do not address his thesis in my chapter.

8.   In spite of its documentary tendencies, Shohat locates *Waltz with Bashir* more generally within the tradition of Palestinian Wave cinema, which is characterised by references to the Arab-Israeli conflict and by presenting Palestine from an Israeli perspective. Shohat's categorisation is based primarily on how focalising in the film is limited to the Israeli viewpoint but there are other aspects that align it to this genre, such as the artistic and creative personality of the main protagonist. See Shohat, *Israeli Cinema*, 230 and 286.

9.   Folman locates himself as a second generation film-maker: 'you can't come from a home of survivors and not be aware of where you come from [...] it influences everything in your life [...] And it's in the movie'. Quoted in Joan Dupont, 'Ari Folman's journey into a heart of darkness,' *The New York Times*, May 19, 2008, http://www.nytimes.com/2008/05/19/arts/19iht-ari.1.13005821.html (accessed March 6, 2011).

10. See Raya Morag, *Waltzing with Bashir: Perpetrator Trauma and Cinema* (London: IB Tauris, 2013)

11. *Waltz with Bashir*, 57:22–58:22.

12. In the English subtitles, 'Luna Park' is translated more generally as 'fairground', Folman, *Waltz with Bashir*, time code 09:53.

13. Yosefa Loshitzky refers to Marianne Hirsch's theory of 'postmemory' in Yosefa Loshitzky, *Identity Politics on the Israeli Screen* (Austin: University of Texas Press, 2001), 15–31. See also Marianne Hirsch, *Family Frames: Photography, Narrative, and Postmemory* (Cambridge and London: Harvard University Press, 1997) and ,more recently, *Hirsch, The Generation of Postmemory: Writing and Visual Culture after the Holocaust* (New York: Columbia University Press, 2013)

14. Ibid., 01:14:37.

Chapter Six: *Waltz with Bashir*'s Reception in Israel and Abroad

Waltz with Bashir is certainly an ideal art house film: it combines 'fashionable' politics (the Israel-Palestine conflict) with dream sequences and hallucinations, all set to the rousing beat of eighties pop. The animation sequences move from 'realistic'– i.e. in a cafe or a friend's house – to those that resemble an acid trip, whilst the live news footage at the end lends a climactic gravitas, inviting the ideal viewer to ponder the nuances of memory and denial and the ambiguous roles of media and journalism. In this sense, it is not surprising that it was so well received by international critics. Its concerns are sufficiently general to appeal to a wide audience and vague enough to be universally accessible. On the other hand these concerns are in a specific enough context (the Middle East) to be seductive and challenging.

Waltz with Bashir's media reception can be loosely categorised into four groups: admiration for Folman's 'bravery'; accusations of hypocrisy; accusations of negative misrepresentation; and praise for the film's representation of war, and war trauma. It is important to stress that there are Arab, Israeli, and Western examples within each group. I shall look at each of these groups more closely, focusing on the media reception in Israel, America, the United Kingdom and the Arab world. By way of conclusion I will also look briefly at the film's scholarly reception.

Admiration

Waltz with Bashir received mostly positive criticism in Israel. It garnered six Israeli academy awards: Best Movie, Best Director, Best Screenplay, Best Artistic Design, Best Editing and Best Sound Design. It was also Israel's entry for Best Foreign Film in the 2009 Oscars. It is notable that the film was so successful in Israel even though the country's part in Sabra and Shatila was a source of conflicting emotions. Indeed, in 1982, following news of the massacres, over 300 000 Israelis demonstrated in protest against the government and the then Defence Minister, Ariel Sharon.

In fact, Folman complained that the film was received 'too well' in Israel:

I was expecting at least a kind of debate – at least a controversy, something...and then I was hugged dearly by all of the political spectrum, the government took it as a project and they keep sending the film all over the world on their expense. I considered myself this really cool rebel and now I'm the government's darling, so it's kind of problematic for me.[1]

Folman acknowledged that the government's support for the film was self-serving as it showed the country to be a tolerant one, one that can withstand criticism. Perhaps disturbingly, David Saranga, the Israeli consul for media and public affairs in New York openly stated:

One of the challenges is that people in the world see Israel as responsible for what happened in Sabra and Shatila, and this movie shows it was Lebanese who killed Palestinians...Second, the fact that the person who is asking the tough questions is an Israeli shows the morality of the Israeli society and the Israeli soldiers...so I don't find it as something that can hurt our public relations, not at all.[2]

It is therefore not surprising if several critics have suggested that the film's overall success in Israel is precisely because it places the country in a positive light; it shows Israel to be thoughtful and sensitive and courageous. *The Christian Science Monitor* called it 'a supremely courageous act not only as a piece of filmmaking, but much more so as a moral testament.'[3] Bradley Burston, writing for *Haaretz* in 2009, gushed: 'In a modern climate of diminished reality and computer-generated truth, the honesty of *Waltz with Bashir* comes as an astonishment.'[4] Similarly, A.O. Scott, writing for the *New York Times* called it 'a work of astonishing aesthetic integrity and searing moral power.'[5] Commenting upon the live footage at the end of the film, Scott wrote: 'This ending shows just how far Mr Folman is prepared to go, not in the service of shock for its own sake, but rather in his pursuit of clarity and truth.'[6] Jonathan Romney (the *Independent*) also praised *Waltz with Bashir* for its courage, writing that it comes across as 'a sincere, personal and deeply painful undertaking that lets neither its maker nor his nation off the hook. It's a brave and necessary film...'.[7]

One of the most enthusiastic reviews for *Waltz with Bashir* can be found, perhaps unexpectedly, in the online publication *The Palestine Chronicle*, which prides itself on not promoting any particular political agenda.

Israeli jazz-musician and novelist, Gilad Atzmon, wrote (rather politically):

> To a certain extent, it is a very brave individual attempt to deal with the
> devastating collective Israeli past...This may explain why the Israelis
> are so enthusiastic about the film. On the one hand, it wasn't them who
> made the actual kill. On the other hand, loving the film portrays them
> as first-rate humanists.[8]

In other words, the film criticises Israel but never blames it for the
massacre. It is just enough criticism to suggest self-reflection, but not
enough to accuse Israel of facilitating genocide. The emphasis in the
film is on what Folman didn't know, rather than on what the Israeli
government and military did know. Furthermore, Atzmon credits *Waltz
with Bashir*'s 'transparency' and makes a bold assertion: 'It seems
that it is actually Israelis and ex-Israelis who are producing the most
eloquent and sharp criticism of Israel, Zionism and the Jewish identity.'[9]
Atzmon is making two points in his review: first, the film is an incisive
critique of Israel's indirect role in the massacre; two, the film's brilliance
permits Israelis to feel proud of themselves as liberal and sensitive souls.
Atzmon's conclusions, of course, depend upon his interpretation of the
film as transparent and honest. Other critics might well argue that the
film was popular in Israel precisely because it wasn't that honest or
transparent.

In Lebanon, where *Waltz with Bashir* was banned due to a nationwide
prohibition on Israeli products, it was still much sought after on the
black market. It was even shown illegally in Beirut in 2009 by UNAM,
an organisation that researches Lebanese history. This illegal viewing,
which demonstrated an unexpected enthusiasm amongst the Lebanese
for an Israeli film, attracted international media attention. In particular,
articles covering the story at the time emphasised the positive reactions
expressed by those that attended the screening. These reactions also
praise the film in terms of courage. The UK's *Guardian* reports:

> Ali Mikdad, a 36-year-old architect who attended the 17 January
> screening, was impressed that Folman's film did not gloss over Israel's
> role in the massacres. 'It shows that Israeli soldiers see what is
> going on inside the camps and they do nothing to stop it' said Mikdad.
> 'Instead, they fired flares so that those committing the crimes could see
> better.'[10]

One journalist reporting from the Sabra refugee camp observed that *Waltz with Bashir* could provoke civil unrest in Lebanon between the Christians and the Muslims: 'In addition to being curious about the Israeli point of view, people are keen to see *Waltz with Bashir* precisely because subjects such as the Sabra and Shatila massacres are still taboo in public discourse.'[11] The journalist quotes one interviewee who confirms this: 'Personally, I am jealous...Jealous that it is the "enemies" who are making the effort to approach the issues that are weighing down on all of us.'[12] Another spectator expressed similar sentiments: 'I envy this Israeli filmmaker because he was able to document a history us Lebanese should have documented.'[13]

Meanwhile, an American academic commentator, in support of Israel's tackling of the subject, wrote that without 'comparable productions from Lebanon, Jordan, Syria, and the Palestinian territories themselves, *Waltz with Bashir* [...] resembles nothing so much as clapping with one hand.'[14]

In this sense, there is admiration for the film because it tackles a subject that other parties (Lebanese Christians and Muslims) fear to broach. Monica Borgmann, who organised the UNAM screening in Beirut, elaborated upon the unexpected interest in the film:

> ...there's a lot of common history between Lebanon and Israel, even if it's a very painful history. The last war was in 2006 and the interest in *Waltz with Bashir* proves what I'm saying – people would like to know the other side. I've no idea if the Israelis are interested to know the Lebanese side, but at least I know that in Lebanon there is a need to confront themselves with the past.[15]

Accusations of hypocrisy

Negative criticism of *Waltz with Bashir* focused a lot on the question of insincerity and bad faith. Meir Schnitzer from the Israeli daily *Ma'ariv* wrote that: 'It was a progressive movie in the way it was presented with the animation, but in its conclusions, social and political, it was more mainstream than (hawkish politician) Shaul Mofaz.'[16] Similarly, the head of screenwriting studies at Tel Aviv University, Kobe Niv, accused the film of letting Israel off the hook and focusing too much on the Phalangists.[17] *The Daily Star Lebanon* also lamented the focus on the Phalangists:

...Bashir leaves you with the impression that Israeli soldiers are nice kids, sacred shitless – contrary to the brutality evinced on television news footage...In Folman's narrative, occupation does not make good people do bad things; rather it makes good people watch bad people (aka 'the Lebanese') do bad things.[18]

On the other hand, in the midst of mostly negative criticism from the Arab press, there were some journalists that defended Folman's depiction of events. Here Egyptian journalist Joseph Fahim elaborates on Folman's disclosure of Israeli culpability and counters the criticism that *Waltz with Bashir* is nothing but Israeli propaganda:

For that matter, I honestly believe it's naive of Arab critics to render the film an Israeli effort to wash the country's hands off the blood of Palestinians. The direct involvement of the Israeli soldiers Arab critics referred to is highly questionable and there's no tangible means of proving it because hardly any footage of the massacre exists.[19]

Israeli journalist, Gideon Levy, whose *Haaretz* review was openly vitriolic, scorned Folman's delayed investigation into an event that had taken place twenty years before, describing it as a typical case of 'we shot and we cried.'[20] In contrast to those critics that interpreted the film as 'honest' Levy claimed that the live footage at the end 'was the first (and last) moment of truth and pain in *Waltz with Bashir*.'[21] Levy's stance is, yes, Israel loves *Waltz with Bashir* and Israelis love *Waltz with Bashir*, but this is only because the film is pure propaganda. He writes:

Hollywood will be enraptured, Europe will cheer and the Israeli Foreign Ministry will send the movie and its makers around the world to show off the country's good side... why do we need propagandists, officers, commentators and spokespersons who will convey 'information'? We have this waltz.[22]

In reference to the actual waltz scene, critic Hillel Halkin wrote:

What terrible things Israel has done – and how wonderful it is to have souls sensitive enough to admit it. A country that knows its Chopin can't be all bad. My friend tells me it's Opus 64.[23]

Halkin's comment is not only sarcastic but quite provocative: the Nazis' love of classical music (Wagner in particular) is often referred to as an indication that cultured and 'evil' are not mutually exclusive. This is especially pertinent in Folman's case because so many scenes with Israeli violence (including the waltz) are set to a score that clearly rouses and entertains the audience. Since the film is a commercial and artistic venture it cannot be otherwise. But Halkin is clearly alluding to the bizarre juxtaposition of the much lauded soundtrack and the accompanying images of Israeli atrocity.

Twitch Film, a website devoted to independent and cult movies, focused on the definition of 'documentary', arguing that *Waltz with Bashir* was anything but. The website was especially brutal in its accusations of propaganda: 'While *Waltz with Bashir* occupies the upper end of the scale in terms of quality filmmaking, it incredibly dominates the lower end of the political propaganda spectrum with its insidiousness...'[24]

Uri Klein, also writing for *Haaretz* offered a slightly more tempered review, acknowledging that it was a 'shooting and crying' sort of film that expresses 'an off-putting degree of coyness, guilt and self-pity.'[25] On the other hand, Klein conceded that the animation, which creates a distance between the audience and the events depicted, prevented the 'coyness, guilt and self pity' from being too embarrassing.[26] Klein doesn't really elaborate on this; but perhaps the point he is making is that the animation distracts the viewer from the film's self-serving message (namely that Folman is traumatised by the massacre, but wasn't responsible) and allows him or her to ponder other more universal questions such as memory and trauma.

Accusations of negative misrepresentation

Waltz with Bashir was released in 2008. At the time of its release, Israel was engaged in the Gaza War – also known as Operation Cast Lead – a three-week conflict between Israel and the Palestinians in the Gaza Strip that took place from December 2008 until January 2009. Ninety per cent of polled Israelis supported the operation. Outside of Israel, the conflict generated heated demonstrations for and against both sides and a UN special mission report found both the Palestinians and the Israelis guilty of war crimes. Meanwhile, at the Golden Globe Awards in January 2009,

Folman neglected to mention the Gaza war during his acceptance speech and was lambasted by critics.

In the midst of this negative publicity, many Israelis felt that *Waltz with Bashir* placed the country and the IDF in an overly negative light, distorting what life was really like for the Israeli soldiers involved. Shoham Nicolet, executive director of the US-based Israeli Leadership Council voiced such concern:

> The concern is the timing...Following the Second Lebanon War and the operation in Gaza, the movie might strengthen a false image of Israel as an aggressive country victimising its enemies. Unfortunately, some of the ideas and vocabulary used in the movie can be taken out of context and might reinforce the misleading anti-Israel propaganda.[27]

In an interview with *Vanity Fair*, two Israeli soldiers, a father and son, argued that the film would give outsiders a one-sided and false image of Israel. The son said that he hated the way the film portrayed Israel and Israeli soldiers while the father also felt that the depiction of the Israeli soldier was exaggerated for artistic effect. The father was also offended by the references to the Shoah:

> I think it's giving a distorted picture. What really bothered me is that he made the connections to the Nazis. I don't think it was appropriate... the Holocaust was a final solution...Here there was a local issue, and it was wrong and I'm condemning it, but it was an issue between the Christians and the PLO.[28]

In fact, the Israeli-Nazi parallels in *Waltz with Bashir* incensed many viewers, leading to accusations of anti-Semitism and Israeli self-hatred. In reference to Ben-Yishai's 'Warsaw liberation' comment, one critic, John Rosenthal, even goes as far as to accuse Folman of modelling the animated image of the little Palestinian boy on the iconic photo from Warsaw. This critic cattily remarks that the Palestinian boy's arms are suspiciously raised in the same way as those of the Jewish boy.[29] Rosenthal concludes his article by suggesting that Folman's film actually provides Germany with a salve for its past:

> Such allusions will be music to the ears and balm for the souls for Folman's European and, more specifically, German audience. What

greater absolution could there be for the horrors inflicted by Germans on Jews during the Second World War than to find that Jews themselves have been complicit in analogous crimes?[30]

Ethan Bronner of the *New York Times* put it more mildly: 'Mention of the Holocaust may jar, since nothing in the story compares with Nazis' systemic multiyear slaughter of millions of Jews in some two dozen countries...'[31]

Of course, accusations of misrepresentation came from the other side as well, with critics concerned that the film indulged its portrayal of the Israeli soldiers while ignoring the Palestinians. This is a fair criticism: the Palestinians in *Waltz with Bashir* are barely noticeable; when we see them they are either dead or, in the case of the live footage, screaming in Arabic without subtitles to rescue them from their 'otherness'. Naira Antoun argues that the representation of Palestinians in the film is completely de-humanising; their only function is to show their effect on the Israelis.[32] Considering the massacre at Sabra and Shatila was perpetrated against the Palestinians, their absence within the film is striking. Antoun also comments on the fact that the Palestinians are associated with the massacre but shut out from the rest of the film's timeline: '...they are frozen in an incomprehensible, and in effect, inaudible, wail.'[33] Similarly, a review of the film on the *Angry Arab News Website*, provocatively titled, 'Dance of Death: *Waltz with Bashir* and Sympathy for the Killer' also picked up on the absence of Palestinians.[34] The author of the review, Asad AbuKhalil, known in the blogosphere as the Angry Arab, compares *Waltz with Bashir* to a painting by Renoir called *The Mosque* (*La Mosquée*, 1881). This painting shows an indeterminate throng of Arabs on a hill near a mosque. AbuKhalil, who is also a professor of Political Science at California State University, argues that the denial of Arab individuality apparent in Renoir's nineteenth-century painting is replicated in Folman's film.[35] He writes: 'They cross into view only fleetingly in order that the viewer won't sense them and so as not to make a relationship between them and the viewer'.[36]

Folman nevertheless stated that it would have been inappropriate to tell the Palestinians story for them. He deliberately focused on the Israelis because this is what he knew. Whilst this is a fair defence, the lack of subtitles during the live footage was picked up by several critics. Folman has not explained why the Arab women remained un-translated. That is, we do not know if he simply wanted to show the original news footage, which may have been un-translated; or, because he wanted to depict his own incomprehension.

Praise for *Waltz with Bashir*'s representation of war and war trauma

In an interview for *J.Weekly.com* Folman stressed his film's universal anti-war message:

> In a way, each country reacted to the film like the history of that country...In France it was about guilt, mainly because of their past in Algeria. In Germany it was all about me doing the comparison of the Holocaust and the massacre.[37]

And in an interview with *The Guardian* he explained that he wanted the film to move beyond its Israeli parameters and show the stupidity of war in general; war 'has no glory, no glamour, no bravery, no brotherhood of men, nothing.'[38] *The San Francisco Chronicle* wrote of the universal archetypes in the film, such as the teenage nerd, and the idolised leader; and that in spite of the historical context, the film was 'telling a bigger story: that war carries a toll on everyone involved, even those who – decades later – might have the superficial trappings of a successful life.' *The Sydney Morning Herald* wrote: 'It is intended as a war film that will make no one want to join up...It takes away all the conventional excitement that make young men think going to war might be fun.'[39]

The Christian Science Monitor wrote:

> And because Folman's odyssey is so all-encompassing, we can connect to it psychologically in ways that transcend the historical particulars of Lebanon in 1982. It's a movie about the wages of suffering, on all sides, in battle.[40]

One of the chief universal messages relayed in the film was that the effect of trauma is both powerful and devastating. *The Wall Street Journal* wrote that Folman's success was in 'charting the human mind's gift at keeping bad memories at bay.'[41] In a similar vein, *Newsweek* said that '*Waltz with Bashir* is about how memory can distort, and shield us, from the truth.'[42]

Alongside praise for the film's representation of trauma was admiration for the use of animation to depict this trauma and the effect it has on memory. Unsurprisingly, Folman's choice to animate *Waltz with Bashir* was of great interest to nearly all critics and reviewers, many of whom commented on other recent works of animation with adult themes such as Richard Linklater's *Waking Life* (2001) and *A Scanner Darkly* (2006). Some also commented on Marjane Satrapi's graphic novel and film *Persepolis* (2000 and 2007 respectively) with the conclusion that animation is no longer just for children.

The independent and avant-garde art magazine, *Soma*, comments on the fact that *Waltz with Bashir* uses at least three types of animation styles and colour palettes to represent the vagaries of memory, specifically memory that has been affected by a traumatic event.[43] Jonathan Romney talks about the 'toxic yellow sky' as 'the film's leitmotif colour';[44] and Kim Nicolini, artist and blogger, writing for cultural website *Bad Subjects*, suggested that:

> ...as Folman gets closer to the truth, the color begins to dissipate from his vision...the film's palette begins to fade from highly stylised color-infused animation into gray realism bordering on documentary photography...[45]

Finally, in view of the film's subject, praise for its representation of war and war trauma is not really surprising. Perhaps what is surprising is that *Waltz with Bashir* had a powerful impact on Israeli war veterans who felt that they were forced to re-live their traumatic experiences in Lebanon. Folman has said in interviews that ever since the film was released strangers have approached him wanting to talk about their memories of Lebanon. He says that the film acts like an itch that they want to scratch.[46] Jewish American War veteran, Tod Norman, wrote a piece in *The Jewish Chronicle* saying that *Waltz with Bashir* helped him to come to terms with his own experiences in Lebanon.[47] Norman, who, like Carmi Canaan, left Israel after the war, wrote that it was only after seeing Folman's film that he found the courage to return. Norman said that it was only after watching the film he realised that he had been repressing strong feelings of shame about his time in Lebanon with the IDF.[48]

Scholarly reception of *Waltz with Bashir*

A quick glance at scholarly work on *Waltz with Bashir* reveals certain trends. It seems that the film's representation of war memory and trauma is of special interest to academics. There are numerous articles and essays focusing on the film's ability to capture, via animation, the psychological impact of war. These include articles: 'Animated Documentary and the Scene of Death: Experiencing *Waltz with Bashir*' by Katrina Schlunke; 'I Witness: Re-presenting Trauma in and by Cinema' by Tamar Ashuri;[49] 'War fantasies: memory, trauma and ethics in Ari Folman's *Waltz with Bashir*' by Raz Yosef;[50] 'Screen Memory in *Waltz with Bashir*' by Garrett Stewart; [51] and 'Loss and mourning: cinema's language of trauma in *Waltz with Bashir*' by N.J. Mansfield.[52] There are also books (though surprisingly few) on the subject including: Raya Morag's *Waltzing with Bashir: Perpetrator Trauma and Cinema*;[53] Selena Ann Dickey's *Animating Trauma: Waltz with Bashir and the Animated Documentary*;[54] and Raz Yosef's *The Politics of Loss and Trauma in Contemporary Israeli Cinema*.[55]

Morag's monograph argues that the recent wave of Israeli documentary cinema, including *Waltz with Bashir*, constitutes a new phenomenon in cinema trauma studies that shifts attention from the victim to the perpetrator. *Waltz with Bashir* presents the trauma of the complicit indirect perpetrator but it does so ambiguously. This is because Folman is forthright about his passivity (he acknowledges that he didn't try and stop the massacres) but cagey about his activity (we only hear at the end that he obeyed his IDF commanders and lit the flares). He expresses trauma but doesn't accept full responsibility for the atrocities.[56] Morag's thesis therefore supports some of the accusations levied at *Waltz with Bashir* in the media.

Katrina Schlunke's excellent article 'Animated Documentary and the Scene of Death' focuses on two issues: the first is memory; the second is the use of animation. Schlunke argues that the film is organised in anticipation of the final scene and that the spectators become unwittingly implicated in the witnessing and then forgetting of the Palestinians plight. In the closing scenes, we witness the actual news footage but then promptly leave the cinema and forget.

Raz Yosef also argues that 'Memory and the very process of remembering' are the key concerns in the film.[57] Yosef's angle, though ultimately different to that of Schlunke, is that the central issue in *Waltz with Bashir* is not to do with what happened in 1982, but how it is remembered. He suggests that the film's focus on the soldiers' personal memory of war indicates the decline of national collective memory in Israel. In this sense the focus is on what the film signifies for Israel and how it marks a landmark in how Israel narrates its wars. Yosef's thesis is unusual in that it hasn't really been replicated in the media. While newspaper reviews have alluded to a variety of topics – memory, the Holocaust, the Vietnam War, the representation of the Palestinian versus the Israeli – there hasn't been anything about why the shift from collective to personal memory should be of significance. This is perhaps because such an observation requires a broader knowledge of Israeli culture. Yosef's article, by way of conclusion, also tackles the ethical implications of using Holocaust memory to relate to events in Lebanon, and this of course was repeatedly broached in the media.[58]

Conclusion

Scholarly reception of a film clearly differs in nature from media reception. The very elements that get lambasted in newspapers – sympathetic portrayal of the Israeli perpetrator, allusions to the Holocaust – are the very same elements that scholars like to get their teeth into. Journalists who usually only see a film once offer an emotive review depending on what affected them the most in the cinema; academics, who will have usually watched and studied the film many times can focus both on what affects them straight away and also on those elements that are less obvious during an initial viewing.

As we can see from this chapter, media reception of *Waltz with Bashir* was fairly emotional: the film ruffled many feathers and pushed several buttons. Critics either gushed about Folman's bravery or they were indignant about his hypocrisy; they were angry that he dared compare Israel to the Nazis or they were angry that Israel was portrayed as the good guy. Other critics rhapsodized about the touching anti-war message in the film whilst others said it was just propaganda.

But it is precisely this ambiguous ethical quality that provokes academic study of the film. Where journalists and bloggers leave off is where the scholars begin. It is fine to say that a film makes you angry or excites you but it is even better to say why and how. And this is what I have been trying to do in this book: to get to the heart of *Waltz with Bashir* and to ask why it has had, and still has, such a powerful effect on the viewer.

References

1. Robert Siegel, 'Filmmaker reflects on *Waltz with Bashir* reception', *NPR* (2008).

2. Tom Tugend and Ben Harris, '*Waltz with Bashir* passed over for Oscar' *Forward* (2009).

3. Peter Rainer, 'Review: *Waltz with Bashir*', the *Christian Science Monitor* (2009).

4. Bradley Burston, '*Waltz with Bashir*: Gaza, and the post-moral world', *Haaretz* (2009).

5. A.O. Scott, 'Inside a veteran's nightmare', *The New York Times* (2008).

6. Scott, Ibid.

7. Jonathan Romney, '*Waltz with Bashir*', the *Independent* (2008)

8. Gilad Atzmon, 'Movie Review: *Waltz with Bashir*', the *Palestine Chronicle* (2008).

9. Atzmon, Ibid.

10. Ben Child, '*Waltz with Bashir* shown in Beirut', *The Guardian* (2009).

11. Abigail Fielding-Smith, 'Waltz with Who? Observations on Censorship', *The New Statesman* (2009).

12. Fielding-Smith, Ibid.

13. Rita Barotta, 'Lebanon will not waltz with Bashir', *Menassat* (2009).

14. Brendan Simms, 'Israel's first 'Vietnam' film', The Social Affairs Unit (2009).

15. Rachelle Kliger, '*Waltz with Bashir* breaks barriers in Arab world', *the Jerusalem Post* (2009).

16. See Dina Kraft, 'War wounds in *Waltz with Bashir*', *The New York Village Voice* (2008).

17. Kraft, Ibid.

18. Jim Quilty, 'What's all the fuss about *Waltz with Bashir?*', *The Daily Star Lebanon* (2009)

19. Joseph Fahim, 'The Reel Estate: Last word on *Waltz with Bashir*', *Daily News Egypt*, (2009).

20. Gideon Levy, 'Antiwar' film *Waltz with Bashir* is nothing but charade', *Haaretz* (2009).

21. Levy, Ibid.

22. Levy, Ibid.

23. Hillel Halkin, 'The *Waltz with Bashir* Two-Step', *Commentary* (March 2009).

24. Agent Wax, '*Waltz with Bashir* review', *Twitch Film* (2009).

25. Uri Klein, 'Shooting and crying, but differently', *Haaretz* (2008).

26. Klein, Ibid.

27. Tugend and Harris, op.cit.

28. John Lopez, 'Two generations of Israeli soldiers react to *Waltz with Bashir*', *Vanity Fair* (2009).

29. John Rosenthal, '*Waltz with Bashir*, Nazi Germany, and Israel', *PJ Media* (2009).

30. Rosenthal, Ibid.

31. Ethan Bronner, 'In search of the soldier in his past', *the New York Times* (2008).

32. Naira Antoun, 'Film review: *Waltz with Bashir*', The Electronic Intifada, (2009).

33. Antoun, Ibid.

34. Asad AbuKhalil, Dance of Death: *Waltz with Bashir* and Sympathy for the Killer', *The Angry Arab News Service* (2009).

35. AbuKhalil, Ibid.

36. AbuKhalil, Ibid.

37. Dan Pine, '*Waltz with Bashir* creator Ari Folman reflects on newfound notoriety,' *J Weekly.com* (2009).

38. Jonathan Freedland, 'Lest we forget', *The Guardian* (2008).

39. Paul Byrnes, '*Waltz with Bashir*', *the Sydney Morning Herald* (2008).

40. Peter Rainer, 'Review: *Waltz with Bashir*', *the Christian Science Monitor* (2009).

41. Joe Morgenstern, 'Animation fires up war documentary Bashir', *The Wall Street Journal* (2008)

42. David Ansen, '*Waltz with Bashir* Review', *Newsweek* (2008)

43. Jesi Khadivi, '*Waltz with Bashir*: A new direction in documentary film making', *Soma* (2009).

44. Romney, Op. Cit.

45. Kim Nicolini, 'Review of *Waltz with Bashir*,' *Bad Subjects* (2009).

46. Jonathan Freedland, 'Lest we forget', *The Guardian* (2008).

47. Tod Norman, 'How a cartoon helped heal a Lebanon veteran', *The Jewish Chronicle* (2008)

48. Norman, Ibid.

49. Tamar Ashuri, 'I Witness: Re-presenting Trauma in and by Cinema', *The Communication Review*, 13.3 (2010), 171-192.

50. Raz Yosef, 'War fantasises: memory, trauma, and ethics in Ari Folman's *Waltz with Bashir*', *Journal of Modern Jewish Studies*, 9.3 (2010), 311-326.

51. Garrett Stewart, 'Screen Memory in *Waltz with Bashir*', *Film Quarterly*, 63.3 (2010), 58-62.

52. N. J. Mansfield, 'Loss and mourning: cinema's language of trauma in *Waltz with Bashir*', *Wide Screen* (2010).

53. Raya Morag *Waltzing with Bashir: Perpetrator Trauma and Cinema*, (London: I.B. Tauris, 2013).

54. Selena Ann Dickey, *Animating Trauma: Waltz with Bashir and the Animated Documentary*, (San Francisco: San Francisco State University Press, 2010).

55. Raz Yosef, *The Politics of Loss and Trauma in Contemporary Israeli Cinema* (Routledge, 2012).

56. Morag, *Waltzing with Bashir*, pp. 132-133.

57. Yosef, 'War fantasises,' op. cit. p. 316.

58. Yosef, 'War fantasies', pp. 322-324.

Conclusion

I started this book with some key questions: why was *Waltz with Bashir* so successful? What does it do as a film? Is it still as relevant today as it was when it first came out in 2008? I think that this book goes a long way to answering these questions. *Waltz with Bashir* struck a chord because it plays with broad themes like war, memory, amnesia and guilt, in an unusual and entertaining way. At the same time, it is framed within a recognizable historical and political setting, namely the Arab-Israeli conflict, which is specific enough to appeal to an interested audience, though vague enough not to overwhelm the spectator with facts and figures. Unlike Folman's two previous films (*Saint Clara* and *Made in Israel*) *Waltz with Bashir* is full of familiar cultural references like eighties pop music, video arcade games, and Hollywood Vietnam movies, which is possibly why it gets international distribution while the other two films are relatively unknown outside of Israel. The protagonists in *Waltz with Bashir* drink shots and smoke spliffs and they have girlfriends that dump them. Even without the specificities of the First Lebanon War the film is an accessible story about young people experiencing traumatic events and repressing them well into adulthood.

As for the third question, I'd say that yes: *Waltz with Bashir* is still as relevant today as it ever was. Since it came out in 2008 nothing comparable has been made by Folman or anyone else. Meanwhile, two years have passed since *The Congress* was released and it's pretty clear that it has joined *Saint Clara* and *Made in Israel* as one of Folman's quirky though less successful ventures. *Waltz with Bashir*'s unique use of animation and documentary features, coupled with its provocative dual investigation of Lebanon and the Holocaust, has no precedent and as yet no other film is quite like it.

In view of the ongoing political situation in Israel and Palestine *Waltz with Bashir* remains significant for those studying the region. Even though it doesn't dwell on historical detail, the basic plot– Israeli veteran trying to remember his role during the Sabra and Shatila massacre – still resonates with critics and scholars alike. When the film came out there was quite a strong emotional response which was often related to the lack of historical detail: some critics felt that it ignored the Palestinian side, some felt that it placed Israel in a bad light; some felt that it was a great anti-war movie, whilst others felt that it was shameless propaganda.

Meanwhile scholars have enjoyed analysing the film further and have looked at different aspects such as representations of guilt and trauma, the interplay of personal and collective memory, the specific choice of animation over live action and the ethical dimensions of documentary. All of these responses still hold true: *Waltz with Bashir* remains an ethically ambivalent film produced in an equally ambivalent manner – fiction with strong documentary elements, all of which is complicated by animation. The film's narrator tells us that the main protagonist is Ari Folman, the film's director; and yet this is an animated version of Folman and therefore quite separate from the live action counterpart. The film is based around interviews yet the interviews are not live but are rather based on a screenplay. The film ends with the suggestion that Folman now remembers everything but the amnesia is just a storytelling device, since throughout the film Folman always knows what he can't remember. In short, nothing is as it seems. Whether this makes *Waltz with Bashir* a rich and engaging experience or an inconclusive and frustrating one, is entirely up to the viewer.

Index

Lightning Source UK Ltd.
Milton Keynes UK
UKOW06f1250280617

304218UK00004B/10/P